Common Witness

Common Witness

A Story of Ministry Partnership between French and North American Mennonites, 1953-2003

by **David Yoder Neufeld**

Common Witness: A Story of Ministry Partnership between French and North American Mennonites, 1953–2003
by David Yoder Neufeld

Copyright © 2016 by Institute of Mennonite Studies
3003 Benham Avenue, Elkhart, Indiana 46517-1999
http://www.ambs.edu/IMS/
All rights reserved

Copublished with Mennonite Mission Network and Éditions de La Talwogne (Bugnon 19, CH-2316 Les Ponts-de-Martel, Suisse, info@talwogne.ch, www.talwogne.ch)
French edition: *Témoignage commun: Histoire d'un partenariat missionaire entre mennonites français et nord-américains, 1953–2003*

Library of Congress Cataloging-in-Publication Data

Names: Neufeld, David Yoder, author.
Title: Common witness : a story of ministry partnership between French and North American Mennonites, 1953-2003 / by David Yoder Neufeld.
Description: Elkhart, IN : Institute of Mennonite Studies, 2016. | Includes index.

Identifiers: LCCN 2016003860 | ISBN 0936273550 (alk. paper)
Subjects: LCSH: Mennonites—France—History—20th century. |
   Mennonites—North America—History—20th century. |
   Mennonites—France—Missions—History—20th century. | Church
   work—France—History—20th century.
Classification: LCC BX8119.F8 N48 2016 | DDC 289.7/440904—dc23
LC record available at http://lccn.loc.gov/2016003860

Printed in the United States of America by Duley Press, Mishawaka, Indiana
Cover designed by Mary E. Klassen; cover art by Myriam Schott, "Living together, with our differences." Used with the gracious permission of Association d'Établissments du Domaine Emmanuel (AEDE)

Photos courtesy of:
Anabaptist Mennonite Biblical Seminary collection: page 76.
Foyer Grebel collection: pages 89, 90, 116, 119, 120, 121, 126, 127, 128, 130, 146, and 151
Jakob and Hotshche Kikkert collection: pages 78, 80, 81, 85, 86, 87, 96, 99, 123, and 124
James Krabill collection: pages 91, 92, and 94
Mennonite Central Committee Photo Archive: pages 2, 4 (photo by C. F. Klassen), 5, 6, and 7
Mennonite Mission Network archives: pages 125, 130, and 134
Robert Witmer collection: pages 15, 20, 23, 24, 25, 26, 27, 28, 29, 31, 36, 39, 43, 44, 45, 46, 47, 52, 53, 54, 59, 60, 61, 63, 64, 68, 69, 70, 101, 102, 104, and 142

Contents

Introduction

On October 5, 1954, French Mennonite leaders Pierre Widmer and Pierre Sommer visited the subprefecture of Montbéliard and established a new association, Mission Mennonite Française (MMF). Their action followed years of discussions with North American representatives of Mennonite Board of Missions and Charities (MBMC), the mission agency of the Mennonite Church (MC), in which these groups had explored the possibility of initiating a collaborative evangelistic effort in France. The creation of MMF, which served as the institutional means to facilitate this cooperation, signaled the beginning of a decades-long intercultural partnership in mission between European and North American Mennonites, who together fashioned a comprehensive and innovative Anabaptist Christian witness in France.

This book documents the origins and development of this partnership. From 1953 to 2003, MMF and MBMC (Mennonite Board of Missions after 1971) worked with each other and with a variety of other partners, most prominently Mennonite Central Committee (MCC), to develop a joint missionary venture. The many fruits of these organizations' efforts occupy a prominent place in this book, which details the founding of three Mennonite congregations in the greater Paris area, the establishment of ministries for youth with developmental disabilities and mental health conditions, the development of ministries for foreign students and for people with social and spiritual needs, and the creation of a center for the study and promotion of Anabaptist theology. The institutional legacy of this partnership has shaped the contemporary Mennonite church in France in important ways. This book adds to the body of historical research on French Mennonites in the twentieth century.

However, this work's primary objective is to recount a story about the relationship between Mennonites divided by linguistic and cultural barriers but united in their call to witness to the gospel. This book exists because those who participated in this missionary project believe that the history of cooperation, negotiation, accommodation, struggle, and shared faith in the power of God and the testimony of Jesus Christ is relevant to the broader church, Mennonite and beyond. By carefully documenting an instance in which missionaries deliberately carried out their work within a framework of partnership, this brief history provides those interested in the church's mission with an example of how such an approach was implemented in one historical case. Without concealing the challenges inherent in this model of missionary work, the following study of cooperation among North American and French Mennonites in France demonstrates some of the benefits that have stemmed from intercultural collaboration in mission, an approach that increasingly animates contemporary thinking about Anabaptist missions.

I come to this project as a relative outsider. Ties of family and friendship to several of the story's protagonists do not lessen the distance between this history's unfolding and my own lived experience. I have attempted to approach research with a critical ear and eye. The voices present in the sources, consciously or unconsciously, pursue certain aims. Whether in oral or documentary form, they rarely reflect past reality unerringly. Thus, whenever possible, I have tried to avoid basing my interpretation on a single source or perspective. To this end I have drawn on MBMC, MBM, and MMF archival materials; private correspondence; and personal interviews with individuals from France, Canada, and the United States. To further understand the perspective of French Mennonites, I have relied heavily on the national church's monthly periodical, *Christ Seul*.[1] In some instances, inevitably, there are silences in the sources. Many of the partnership's earliest participants have died. In other cases, archival documents have not been readily available. Yet, to some extent, these documentary gaps make this history possible. As historian John Arnold explains, "If there were no problems with discovering what happened in the past, there would be no need for historians, and thus no history—just 'what happened' without dispute or question."[2] In other words, the fact that elements of the story remain open to question makes the past a subject

---

1 French historian Jean Séguy attests to the historiographical trustworthiness of *Christ Seul*. Jean Séguy, *Les Assemblées Anabaptistes-Mennonites de France* (Paris: Mouton & Co, 1977), 649.

2 John H. Arnold, *History: A Very Short Introduction* (New York: Oxford University Press, 2000), 78–79.

of study rather than self-evident truth. Thus, what follows is not a definitive account. There are always new questions to be asked, though I have tried to ask the most pertinent ones.

I cannot claim to be a disinterested observer of this history of partnership. As a practicing Mennonite interested in the testimony and growth of the church, I am invested in the manner in which this story is portrayed. Through my attempts to produce as fair an account as possible, I have become increasingly convinced of this story's importance. It is my hope that this presentation will create similar sentiments in the reader. In the interests of clarity, this history of partnership is developed over three chapters, which detail its beginnings, maturation and growth, and conclusion, respectively. The account is bookended by an introductory chapter that describes the conditions out of which the collaborative effort emerged and a final chapter that brings together participants' reflections on the partnership's lasting significance.

Throughout all stages of the preparation of this book, I received continuous support and wise counsel from each member of a supervisory committee composed of Neal Blough, James Krabill (chair), Art Neuenschwander, Emma Peterschmitt, Wilbert Shenk, and Robert Witmer. I offer particular thanks to Robert for overlooking my scholarly inexperience and entrusting to me the telling of this story. From France, André Hege and Neal Blough kindly provided me with archival materials from the Association d'Établissements du Domaine Emmanuel and the Centre Mennonite de Paris, respectively. Thanks to James Krabill for the many hours he spent in assembling the photos and captions that illustrate the text. I am grateful to Barbara Nelson Gingerich for preparing the manuscript for publication, to Naomi Yoder and George and Agnes Epp for their research assistance, and to Rebecca and Tom Yoder Neufeld for their editorial suggestions and personal encouragement. Special thanks to you, Gina, for your patience and love. I dedicate my work to Anne Marie Yoder (née Guth), who has shown me the richness and the sacrifice that belong to intercultural partnership.

1
Preconditions for Partnership
European and North American Mennonites Reconnect, 1917–52

The shared desire of European and North American Mennonites to initiate cooperative mission work in France grew out of the reintroduction of these two constituencies to each other in the first half of the twentieth century. Over the course of the previous 100 years, 15,000 Mennonites emigrated from Europe to North America.[1] Transatlantic relationships were maintained through ongoing migration and correspondence between family and friends. Yet, with the passage of time, a gradual loss of cultural and linguistic commonalities contributed to a weakening of the tenuous ties that linked these groups together.[2]

North American Mennonite Relief Work in Europe

War transformed these patterns of interaction by inducing the return of North Americans to Europe. This return, while "characterized by a diversity of motivations, goals, organizational sponsorship, and geographical destinations," took the form of a response to the material consequences of the period's horrific conflicts.[3] In 1917, following the entry of the United States into World War I, Mennonite Board of Missions and Charities collected donations for war relief and channeled them to Europe through Mennonite Relief Commission for War Sufferers (MRCWS). Administered under the auspices of American Friends Service Committee (AFSC), these funds supported some fifty North

---

1 J. Robert Charles, "North American Mennonite Agencies in Europe since World War II," *Mission Focus* 3 (1988): 48.

2 Neal Blough, "Mission Efforts in Europe: New Congregations, New Questions," in *Testing Faith and Tradition*, ed. John A. Lapp and C. Arnold Snyder (Intercourse, PA: Good Books, 2006), 233.

3 Charles, "North American Mennonite Agencies in Europe," 48.

American Mennonite reconstruction workers stationed primarily in France.[4]

From 1937 to 1939, North American Mennonite support for relief work in Europe extended into Spain, which had been debilitated by civil war. Mennonite Relief Committee (MRC), created by MBMC as a successor organization to MRCWS, believed the most appropriate missionary reaction to conditions in Spain to be a peace witness, manifested through distribution of food and clothing. This response to the physical needs of the population vitally expressed Christian love and thus formed an essential element of a comprehensive evangelistic program. The committee assumed that

A North American Mennonite delegation visiting a day nursery administering a child feeding program in Lyon, France (ca. 1941). Left to right: Ernest Bennett (at door), the American consul (standing center), Henry Wiens (kneeling) and Samuel Ybargoyen (the Uruguayan Consul to Vichy in Lyon, who with his wife was helpful to Mennonite Central Committee workers in France). The woman at the door is likely Mrs. Ybargoyen.

communication of the gospel would accompany MRC personnel's relief work.[5]

---

4 Guy F. Hershberger, "Mennonite Relief Commission for War Sufferers (Mennonite Church)," *Global Anabaptist Mennonite Encyclopedia Online*; http://www.gameo.org/encyclopedia/contents/M467133.html. For an account of the repercussions of this reconstruction effort for North American volunteers and the (Old) Mennonite Church (MC), see Anna Showalter, "The Mennonite Young People's Conference Movement, 1919–1923: The Legacy of a (Failed?) Vision," *Mennonite Quarterly Review* 85, no. 2 (2011): 191–99.

---

5 Guy F. Hershberger, *The Mennonite Church in the Second World War* (Scottdale, PA: Mennonite Publishing House, 1951), 195; and Gerlof Homan, " 'Ayuda a los Niños':

Mennonite involvement in Spain provided Mennonites with valuable experience on which they drew in response to the devastation of World War II, a conflict that brought about the greatest expansion of North American Mennonite assistance to war victims in Europe.[6] In this effort, MRC worked under the administration of Mennonite Central Committee, a much larger agency that immediately established programs in Poland, unoccupied southern France, and London.[7] In the years following the war, MCC brokered the presence of North American Mennonites in Europe, with few exceptions. From its postwar headquarters in Basel, Switzerland, MCC directed projects in most of the continent's countries, focusing its efforts on facilitating emergency food and clothing relief, resettling refugees, and reconstructing buildings.[8]

Relief Efforts in France

While MCC policy called for provision of relief to needy people regardless of nationality, creed, and political persuasion, its actions in France intended to serve and stimulate local Mennonites.[9] This work centered on distribution of food and clothing. French Mennonite war victims benefited directly from this aid, which was also channeled through Chalet aux Fleurs and Mont des Oiseaux, two children's homes established in Nancy and Wissembourg, respectively, in 1945. The Mennonite community in Wissembourg also benefited from a twelve-person builders unit, assembled by MCC to repair war-damaged homes.[10] Initially, the organization carried out these activities unilaterally. However, after several years of working without clear links to French Mennonites, MCC intentionally created opportunities for cooperation.

MCC's strategy in France responded to reports from its own personnel who described French Mennonites as somewhat disunited, isolated, and

Mennonite Relief Work in Spain, 1937–1939," *Mennonite Quarterly Review* 86, no. 3 (2012): 357.

6 Homan, "Ayuda a los Niños," 370.

7 Guy F. Hershberger, "Relief Work," *Global Anabaptist Mennonite Encyclopedia Online*; http://www.gameo.org/encyclopedia/contents/R4594ME.html.

8 Charles, "North American Mennonite Agencies in Europe," 49.

9 Michel Paret, "L'Action Sociale Mennonite en France au XX° Siècle: Approches Diachronique et Analytique" (PhD diss., École Pratique des Hautes Études, Sorbonne, Paris, 1997), 203.

10 Hershberger, *The Mennonite Church*, 201.

Orie O. Miller (right), Mennonite Central Committee Executive Secretary, and Michael Robert (M. R.) Zigler, Executive Secretary of Brethren Service Committee, collaborate on postwar relief efforts at this 1945 meeting in Paris.

without interest in relief work outside their own communities.[11] While these evaluations could be dismissed as the ingenuous observations of recently arrived foreigners, they reflected the existing state of French Mennonitism in a number of ways. At the time, French Mennonites were divided into French- and German-speaking conferences, both loose federations that held no jurisdiction over the internal affairs of member congregations. The absence of a central decision-making body contributed to a lack of formal interaction with other European Mennonites or North American Mennonite organizations.[12] Furthermore, many French congregations were wary of engagement in the public sphere. Although they had appointed deacons to organize their response to members of their communities in need of assistance in the past, most now viewed this task as the responsibility of the French state.[13] Last, the primary preoccupation of many French Mennonites was to recover from the trauma and disruption the recent conflict had inflicted on their families, congregations, and property.

---

11 Paret, "L'Action Sociale Mennonite," 190.

12 Ibid., 85.

13 Ernest Hege, e-mail message to author, 14 July 2012.

As MCC became aware of these circumstances, the organization expressed a desire to establish lasting connections with French Mennonites, to stimulate theological reflection among them, and to ensure the durability of its own relief work.[14] Concerned about the future of the children's homes, MCC workers became convinced that local Mennonite congregations could best provide the committed Christian personnel needed to guarantee the homes' long-term viability.[15] In October 1946, MCC France director H. P. Buller formally appealed for French collaboration.[16] In response, local Mennonites invited representatives from all congregations of both conferences to meet at Chalons-sur-Saône to discuss the North American proposal. The gathering resulted in the formation of Comité Mennonite de Secours (Mennonite Relief Committee). After several years of dialogue, the committee agreed to support the relocation of the Chalet aux Fleurs to an area closer to most French Mennonite congregations.[17]

Maison de Convalescents in Canet-Plage, France (1942)

14 Paret, "L'Action Sociale Mennonite," 205.

15 Ibid., 181.

16 Jean Séguy, *Les Assemblées Anabaptistes-Mennonites de France* (Paris: Mouton & Co, 1977), 630.

17 Ernest Hege, e-mail message to author, 14 July 2012.

In 1950, Association Mennonite Fraternel (Mennonite Fraternal Association), set up by Comité de Secours to administer the home, used MCC funds to acquire a property outside the town of Valdoie. The Villa des Sapins, as the property was named, later joined Mont des Oiseaux under French Mennonite control. The center became a meeting place for youth, ministers, and church workers; it also became the new headquarters of MCC in France. The exercise in cooperation that resulted in the Valdoie home's establishment and operation served to draw together Mennonite groups distanced by historical circumstances, and it amplified the scope of French Mennonite social activity.[18] It reintegrated the French into broader Mennonite circles and demonstrated to all parties involved the potential fruits of North American and European collaboration.[19]

Transition from Relief to Missionary Work, 1950-52

North American Mennonite Missionaries Follow MCC into Europe

Mennonite Central Committee relief work after World War II introduced many North American Mennonites to the European context. The conditions they encountered convinced them that a continued presence in Europe was justified. Increasingly, MCC envisioned its personnel being replaced by workers sent by Mennonite mission boards. As relief efforts waned, the continued presence of North Americans in Europe moved in a more "spiritual" and less "material" direction.[20]

18 Séguy, *Les Assemblées Anabaptistes-Mennonites*, 633.

19 Ibid., 634.

20 Blough, "Mission Efforts in Europe," 236.

Mennonite relief for children at Maison de Convalescents in Villa St. Christophe, Canet-Plage, France (ca. 1942)

On the basis of the lessons of its recent experience, MCC believed that the initiation of any missionary endeavors should be preceded by consultation with local Mennonites. To promote this end, in the summer of 1950 MCC sponsored a study tour for representatives of six North American mission agencies. Accompanied by MCC Europe staff, delegates conversed with Mennonite leaders from Germany, the Netherlands, Switzerland, and Luxembourg, who expressed interest in further North American assistance and future

Boys in dining room at Maison de Convalescents in Villa St. Christophe, Canet-Plage, France (ca. 1942)

collaboration.[21] MCC, given its established presence in Europe and the relationships it had cultivated, offered to serve as the primary channel of future communication between North American and European Mennonites, while it directed its focus toward strengthening its peace testimony on the continent. As for all "non-Mennonite" areas of Europe, the study tour recommended freedom of activity for foreign mission boards.[22] By 1953, Mennonite agencies had established eight missions on the continent.[23]

MBMC Initiates Missionary Work in Belgium

Mennonite Board of Missions and Charities, one of the agencies participating in the study tour, chose to begin its work in Belgium precisely because of that country's distance from European Mennonites who, the board understood, "may not fully appreciate an evangelistic work within their territory by a foreign branch of their denomination."[24] As was the case elsewhere, Mennonite agency work in Belgium followed the pattern of

21 Ibid., 249.

22 Ibid., 250.

23 Ibid., 237.

24 Charles, "North American Mennonite Agencies in Europe," 49.

transition from humanitarian assistance to spiritual formation. MBMC had foreseen this shift as early as 1943, when a missions committee report stated that "inasmuch as we look to relief work as the possible beginning of permanent mission work, it is our concern that the utmost care be exercised in the choice of personnel so that the impacts made in the work will be Christian and truly Mennonite and will pave the way for the opening of permanent missions."[25] One year after the arrival of a small MRC relief and reconstruction team in Belgium in 1946, a Belgian Mission Study Committee report recommended that missionaries be sent to the country as soon as possible "so that the mission effort in Belgium may capitalize to the full upon the relief effort of that country."[26] The initiative was approved in 1949, and missionaries David and Wilma Shank arrived in Brussels in September 1950.

MBMC missionaries sent to Europe in the 1950s represented a church conference in the process of amplifying its missionary vision. Increased reflection within the Mennonite Church on the missionary endeavor of sixteenth-century Anabaptism, by authors such as Franklin Littell, contributed to a generalized belief that the missionary reach of the conference was insufficient.[27] This realization encouraged increased financial contributions to missions and saw a growing number of young people willing to offer themselves for missionary service.[28]

This postwar missionary awakening among North American Mennonites coincided with what Allen Koop has called the "greatest expansion in the history of missions," spurred primarily by efforts of North American evangelical missionaries around the globe.[29] The causes for this explosion in missionary activity were diverse, including but not limited to dissatisfaction with the approaches of established, theologically liberal mission boards, and the growth of US influence in the postwar world. The increasing strength of evangelical missions manifested itself most clearly in newly independent

---

25 *Report of the Thirty-seventh Annual Meeting of the M.B.M.C.* (1943), 17. Quoted in Hershberger, *The Mennonite Church*, 165–66.

26 Charles, "North American Mennonite Agencies in Europe," 49.

27 Wilbert Shenk, e-mail message to author, 23 August 2012.

28 Hershberger, *The Mennonite Church*, 285–86.

29 Allen V. Koop, *American Evangelical Missionaries in France 1945–1975* (Lanham, MD: University Press of America, 1986), 9.

nations in Africa, Asia, and Latin America. Yet, growing concern for missions also led North Americans to consider Europe a potential mission field for the first time.[30]

Mennonite missionaries arriving in Europe during this period formed part of this movement. Although often differing from their evangelical colleagues in theology and in practice, many Mennonites shared with them a negative view of the spiritual state of Europe and feared that local religious institutions were ill equipped to address the situation.[31] While these attitudes appeared—and sometimes were—condescending and arrogant, they also reflected the views of some Europeans who were alarmed by what they saw as the debilitating impact of violence and secularization on European Christianity. In French churches, a worried minority was struck by "the pervasive de-Christianization of French society."[32] Protestant social scientist Jacques Ellul distilled their concerns, arguing that in the emerging post-Christian society, "Christian concerns became simply irrelevant, and Christian words (piety, salvation, grace, redemption) awaken no echo in the modern French mind."[33] For Ellul, all that remained of Christianity was a

> morality with which everyone is familiar. . . . Post-Christian society, therefore, is not simply a society which followed upon Christendom. It is a society which is no longer Christian, a society that has had the experience of Christianity, is the heir of the Christian past, and believes it has full knowledge of the Christian religion because it retains vague memories of it and sees remnants of it all around. Nothing new, surprising, or unexpected, above all nothing relevant to modern life can come from Christianity; the church and the faith are simply vestiges from the past.[34]

In Belgium, the Shanks experienced this reality firsthand. David Shank, like other young North American Mennonite thinkers living in Europe at the time, had been heavily influenced by the writings of Harold S. Bender, who had encouraged Mennonites to consider "how [their] theology, ethics and mission could come

---

30 Ibid., 7–9.

31 Blough, "Mission Efforts in Europe," 247; and Koop, *American Evangelical Missionaries*, 5.

32 Koop, *American Evangelical Missionaries*, 21.

33 Jacques Ellul, *The New Demons* (New York: Seabury Press, 1975), 24.

34 Ibid., 25.

to terms with twentieth century Western culture."[35] After eighteen months of work in Brussels, Shank authored "A Missionary Approach to Dechristianized Society," a "pioneering" essay based on his experience in Europe.[36] In many ways, it presaged the approaches and actions of MBMC mission efforts in French-speaking Europe over the course of its partnership with MMF.

In the article, Shank portrays the church as the bearer of a basic message, the gospel. This message is conservative to the extent that it judges all human activity in relation to God's unchanging revelation in Jesus Christ. Yet this reality does not excuse the conservatism of the church, which "by nature, origin, and calling is a dynamic creative force." Shank sees the shock of dechristianization as the impetus required to elicit the church's true character. Dechristianized society's rejection of Christendom, a religious, political, and social system imposed by force, offers an opportunity for the church to again become a "vehicle of [the] constant flow of creative power into individual lives." This is the only method by which the church can prove that God's initial revelation continues to be true. In light of these circumstances, Shank contends, "dechristianized society does not in general recognize 'professional' missionaries, and a large part of it looks with suspicion and scorn at 'agents' of the church." Thus, "it is only as an integral part of formal society, as one who is 'in the world'—who has identified himself with society in the modern sense of the word—that a missionary is qualified to bear the message."[37] In order to position itself authentically in the world, Shank argues, the church "is required to remain sensitive to the currents of thought and attitude present in society, and must freely adapt its methods to the conditions of that society."[38]

Shank's call found partial expression in MBMC policy, which tried to prevent the export of "American cultural baggage" by granting its missionaries ample time for language, historical, and cultural studies

35 Blough, "Mission Efforts in Europe," 247–48.

36 Alan Kreider, "West Europe in Missional Perspective: Themes from Mennonite Mission, 1950–2004," in *Evangelical, Ecumenical, and Anabaptist Missiologies in Conversation: Essays in Honor of Wilbert R. Shenk*, ed. James R. Krabill, Walter Sawatsky, and Charles E. Van Engen (Maryknoll, NY: Orbis, 2006), 208.

37 David A. Shank, "A Missionary Approach to a Dechristianized Society," *Mennonite Quarterly Review* 28, no. 1 (1954): 52.

38 Ibid.

before they began their work as evangelists.[39] This policy demonstrated awareness that missionaries worked in a politically charged postwar world characterized by the expansion of US power. Missionaries would be viewed as representatives of their country of origin, the board assumed. The evangelistic message of North American missionaries was not intended to further the claims of a specific political and economic system, but rather, in Shank's estimation, to be their "judge."[40] This approach contrasted distinctly with the majority of other evangelical missions, exemplified by Greater Europe Mission and its leader, retired US Navy chaplain Robert Evans. North American missionary efforts often demonstrated a parochial lack of respect for local sensitivities, an attitude that one MBMC administrator described as counterproductive and embarrassing.[41]

In Brussels, the Shanks adapted to local circumstances in a number of ways. Initially, they continued to distribute food and clothing to Eastern European refugees

as MRC personnel had done since 1946. Soon relationships first developed by MRC personnel drew the couple toward leadership of the administration and operation

David and Wilma Shank related to the Paris initiative from Brussels, Belgium, where they began work in September 1950.

of a local Protestant children's home. They cultivated contacts with local believers, most fruitfully with the Belgian evangelist Jules Lambotte and his French wife,

39 Orley Swartzentruber to Robert Witmer, "The Beginnings of the Work at La Butte Rouge," 21 January 2005, personal files of Robert Witmer, Cambridge, ON.

40 Shank, "A Missionary Approach," 49.

41 Wilbert Shenk, interview by David Neufeld, 1 June 2012.

Madeleine. In response to Pierre Widmer's preaching in France, Madeleine had become a Christian, and on the couple's return to Brussels, they made contact with the Shanks. Jules and a number of his friends from a Protestant youth center in the city shared the missionaries' pacifist convictions and, along with the Shanks, formed the nucleus of the country's first Mennonite congregation, Foyer Fraternel, founded in 1953. For the congregation's inauguration, the group invited Widmer to present a series of evangelistic lectures to which local Protestants were invited. Meanwhile, a member of the children's home's administrative council asked David Shank to lead a Sunday afternoon "cottage" Bible study at his home. Eight members of the group, from "Catholic, Communist and atheist background," asked to be baptized and became the first members of a second Mennonite congregation, founded in a town outside Brussels in 1955.[42]

The Origins of a Missionary Partnership in France

An opportunity to initiate MBMC missionary activity in France emerged shortly after the Shanks began their ministry in Belgium. MCC staff in France, like their counterparts in other parts of Europe, were considering how best to capitalize on years of relief work and were exploring how this could be done in partnership with local Mennonites. In October 1951, MCC France director John H. Yoder authored a report arguing that the "door was open and the way prepared" for mission work in France. Discussions about this possibility had "been in the air" for more than two years, but as relief efforts came to a close it was increasingly clear that "the social service program of MCC is incomplete if it does not lead that way [toward mission work], and in the long run will be hypocritical if it points that way without advancing." Yoder was convinced that French Mennonites would welcome such activity, especially if North American projects would open up service and mission positions for French youth. "One thing that the French, including Pierre Widmer, emphasize is that if americans [sic] attempt mission work in France the actual spearhead of evangelism should be a french [sic] person. This serves only to emphasize the interest, in case one contemplates mission activity in France, of not

---

42 Wilma Shank, interview by David Neufeld, 17 May 2012; and Wilma Shank, e-mail message to author, 12 July 2012.

letting a good available person get away," Yoder suggested.[43]

It is unsurprising that Yoder evaluated French Mennonite attitudes toward missionary activity in France positively, given that his conclusions were drawn from his conversations with Widmer. Then editor of the influential *Christ Seul* and member of the Montbéliard congregation, Widmer had emerged as one of the French Mennonite community's most prominent postwar voices. Through conference meetings and the editorial page of *Christ Seul*, he had attempted to guide local Mennonites toward a rediscovery of their Anabaptist identity, advocating the development of a Mennonite church "that is a truly fraternal community, based on the Word, practicing the priesthood of all believers and determined to proclaim the Gospel."[44] His passion for missions found several avenues of expression, including Comité Mennonite Français de Mission (French Mennonite Mission Committee),

an organization oriented to overseas mission activity for which he served as president from the time of its founding in November 1950.

Widmer's support for North American mission work in France originated in informal discussions with his second cousin, J. D. Graber, general secretary of MBMC from 1944 to 1967, held while Widmer attended the 1948 Mennonite World Conference (MWC) in the United States as a delegate of the French conference.[45] The result of these conversations was a clear understanding on the part of each that he had discovered a willing and trustworthy partner—this despite the fact that they represented Mennonite groups that differed drastically both in size and in the sophistication of their mission institutions.

Graber believed that the opportunity for mission work in France, with its potential for collaboration with local Mennonites, was unique and worth pursuing. His tenure as general secretary coincided with the acceleration of Mennonite mission activity worldwide. Graber exerted strong influence on MBMC mission policy, taking clear steps to address the primary concern that his own experience as a missionary in India

43 John Howard Yoder, "Report on Mission Possibilities in France," 5 October 1951. Box 2. Mennonite Board of Missions Office of the Secretary Overseas and Home Mission Correspondence, 1941–1964. IV/18/010, Mennonite Church USA Archives, Goshen, IN.

44 Séguy, *Les Assemblées Anabaptistes-Mennonites*, 670–71.

45 Ibid., 628.

had raised—namely, the close relationship between Protestant missions and the political and social structures of the colonial states in which they operated. He promoted the "indigenization" of mission projects, which involved eventual transfer of control of missionary projects to local hands. Under Graber's leadership, this policy was to be applied to all future MBMC programs.[46]

That France itself remained a colonial power did not present a challenge to this model. Instead, it was MBMC's hope that the presence of Mennonites in France would facilitate the model's implementation by providing personnel and administrative structures. Thus, soon after they received Yoder's report, Graber and fellow administrator L. C. Hartzler traveled to eastern France, where they visited the children's homes and conversed with Widmer. The report of their visit confirmed not only that France was an attractive mission field but also that French Mennonites would appreciate the North Americans' cooperation and fellowship.

The report's authors envisioned employing French Mennonite workers with doctrinal positions they considered sound. The personnel would be instructed to plant churches that would become independent and self-supporting as soon as possible. Such congregations could be integrated into a French-speaking Mennonite conference that, because of its flexible structure, would tolerate faith communities with views and practices in line with MBMC understandings. A single North American missionary couple "would serve as teacher, preacher, and as advisor to French workers." The report identified the Parisian suburb of Le Raincy and the industrial city of Clermont-Ferrand as potential mission locations, the former because of family ties to children boarding at Mont des Oiseaux and the latter because of its socioeconomic composition. However, Graber and Hartzler recommended that MBMC personnel in Belgium continue to study opportunities in France "and suggest to us specific steps to be taken from time to time in carrying out the program."[47]

46 Wilbert Shenk, interview by David Neufeld in Waterloo, ON, 1 June 2012; and Wilbert R. Shenk, "Graber, Joseph Daniel (1900–1978)," *Global Anabaptist Mennonite Encyclopedia Online*, http://www.gameo.org/encyclopedia/contents/G724.html.

47 J. D. Graber and L.C. Hartzler, "Report on France," 1951. Mennonite Board of Missions Office of the Secretary Overseas and Home Mission Correspondence, 1941–1964. IV/18/010, Mennonite Church USA Archives, Goshen, IN.

Orley and Jane Swartzentruber and family (1950s)

Earlier that year, Orley and Jane Swartzentruber had joined the Shanks in Brussels, tasked with a vaguely defined mission to plant a Mennonite church in French-speaking Europe that was "self-supporting, self-governing and self-propagating."[48] Orley joined

David Shank and John H. Yoder on an exploratory trip to Paris in May 1952. After meeting with Widmer, the workers confirmed that "the best way for Americans to serve is by aid and cooperation with European workers." Given existing commitments in Belgium, the initiation of work in Paris would mean that "one of the families here at Brussels now, would go to France for that work, and the other family would stay in Brussels for the program, never being so far apart from each other for counsel, aid, and cooperative sharing of work."[49] MBMC decided to act on this recommendation, and submitted its decision to initiate mission work in France to the French Mennonite Mission Committee in October.[50] On New Year's Eve, 1952, the Swartzentrubers arrived in Paris, where they soon took up residence in the servants' quarters of a luxury apartment not far from the Arc de Triomphe.[51] They immediately

48 Orley Swartzentruber to Robert Witmer, "The Beginnings of the Work at La Butte Rouge," 21 January 2005, personal files of Robert Witmer, Cambridge, ON.

49 David Shank to J. D. Graber, 24 May 1952. Mennonite Board of Missions Office of the Secretary Overseas and Home Mission Correspondence, 1941–1964. IV/18/010, Mennonite Church USA Archives, Goshen, IN.

50 Séguy, *Les Assemblées Anabaptistes-Mennonites*, 656.

51 Orley Swartzentruber to Robert Witmer, "The Beginnings of the Work at La Butte Rouge," 21 January 2005, personal files of Robert Witmer, Cambridge, ON.

began to lay the groundwork for what would become an exceptional and productive collaborative missionary venture in France.

2
"It Was Natural That We Made Contact"
Partnership Begins, 1953–65

Beginnings in the Région Parisienne, 1953-54

During Orley and Jane Swartzentruber's first year in Paris, Orley looked persistently for a permanent location to begin evangelistic work.[1] André Goll, a young French Mennonite, joined him in this search. The two first explored prospects in Le Raincy, where Mennonite students attending the Bible Institute of Nogent-sur-Marne were evangelizing door-to-door.[2] Swartzentruber and Goll organized several meetings and Bible studies in the neighborhood, but these events elicited little response. In addition, the mission attempted to convene Mennonite families dispersed throughout Paris and its surroundings. This action was taken in response to the recommendation of Pierre Widmer, who had received frequent requests for information about Mennonite places of worship in the area.[3] For a number of years, on the first Sunday of every month, meetings were held at 21, rue de la Baume in the city's eighth arrondissement. Although the group discussed the possibility of starting a church, few participants were willing to formally cut ties with their home congregations in eastern France.[4]

Despite these early frustrations, the missionaries were convinced that the doors remained open for the establishment of a church in the city. Orley later reflected, "As in all missionary work, the missionaries

1 "Paris," *Christ Seul*, December 1953, 10.
2 Jean Séguy, *Les Assemblées Anabaptistes-Mennonites de France* (Paris: Mouton & Co, 1977), 657.
3 Ibid., 656.
4 André Goll, "Région Parisienne—Une Semaine à Paris," *Christ Seul*, January 1956, 31–32.

contribute but one element to the tableau. There is always another element, which is the prevenient work of God, the 'evangelical preparation' as some early Christians referred to it. The promised 'new things' begin to flower when both currents meet."[5]

The "new thing" in Paris, the city's first Mennonite congregation, grew out of Swartzentruber's relationship with Reformed pastor André Trocmé. André and his wife, Magda, had gained renown for sheltering Jews in the southern French village of Le Chambon during the Nazi occupation of France.[6] After the war, they moved to Versailles, where André directed the International Fellowship of Reconciliation. In 1953 Trocmé visited Scottdale, Pennsylvania, where he learned of the Mennonite missionary couple in Paris.[7] On his return, he sought out the Swartzentrubers, seeing the creation of a Mennonite church in the area as a support to his own work.[8]

In October 1953, Trocmé introduced Orley to Anne Sommermeyer. Sommermeyer was a Jew from eastern Germany who had fled to Paris with her husband Hans in 1933 soon after Adolf Hitler assumed power.[9] Following her release from Nazi detention after the German occupation of northern France, Sommermeyer escaped to Le Chambon, where she became a Christian through the wartime ministry of the Trocmés. After the war, Sommermeyer returned to the French capital. Now a member of a local Reformed church, she invited Swartzentruber to lead a multidenominational Bible study. These apartment meetings, held on Friday evenings, took place in the rapidly expanding *cité-jardin* of the Butte-Rouge in the southern suburb of Châtenay-Malabry.[10]

5 Orley Swartzentruber to Robert Witmer, "The Beginnings of the Work at La Butte Rouge," 21 January 2005, personal files of Robert Witmer, Cambridge, ON.

6 For an account of the Trocmé's wartime ministry in Le Chambon, see Philip Hallie, *Lest Innocent Blood Be Shed: The Story of the Village of Le Chambon and How Goodness Happened There* (New York: Harper & Row, 1979).

7 Assemblée Évangélique Mennonite du Foyer Fraternel, congregational history (1956–84), given to Robert and Lois

Witmer, undated, personal files of Robert Witmer, Cambridge, ON.

8 Orley Swartzentruber to Robert Witmer, "The Beginnings of the Work at La Butte Rouge," 21 January 2005, personal files of Robert Witmer, Cambridge, ON.

9 Anne Sommermeyer, "Un itinéraire," *Esprit* 343 (1965): 841.

10 Assemblée Évangélique Mennonite du Foyer Fraternel, congregational history (1956–84), given to Robert and Lois

The Butte-Rouge Bible Study Group

The genesis of the Butte-Rouge Bible study group dates to 1946, when Sommermeyer met the Humbert family on the metro on her way to a Good Friday service in Paris. The Humberts put Sommermeyer in touch with M. Viollier, a Reformed pastor in nearby Montrouge, who introduced her to several Protestant families in Châtenay-Malabry. Beginning in the fall, she organized a small group which met regularly to study the Bible. By 1948, the group had organized a monthly Sunday morning worship service at the Humbert home. On Thursday afternoons, the time which the state had reserved for Christian education, participant Madame Boeckholt welcomed the group's children into her home for biblical lessons. Soon afterward, M. Chatelain joined Anne Sommermeyer in selling Bibles and making personal contacts at a local market.[11] Given its origins, the group might have associated itself with the Reformed church in Montrouge, but because of its desire for a building and, more importantly, Sommermeyer's pacifist sympathies, which she attributed to the teaching of André Trocmé, she contacted Swartzentruber instead.[12]

The study group warmly welcomed Swartzentruber who, beginning in November 1953, "began to work with the group pursuing the study of the New Testament, mainly book by book."[13] The group was composed of a dozen participants, half Protestant, others with marginal Christian backgrounds who maintained an interest in religious philosophy or late medieval mysticism. Swartzentruber's direction led some of these members to abandon the group, while a number of other Protestants joined. In Swartzentruber's view, these meetings resulted "from the fervor and devotion of a few individuals who wish to share their witness with those around them."[14] He saw the group as the nucleus of a future congregation.[15]

Witmer, undated, personal files of Robert Witmer, Cambridge, ON.

11 Ibid.

12 Séguy, *Les Assemblées Anabaptistes-Mennonites*, 657; and Robert Witmer, e-mail message to author, 5 October 2012.

13 Orley Swartzentruber to Robert Witmer, "The Beginnings of the Work at La Butte Rouge," 21 January 2005, personal files of Robert Witmer, Cambridge, ON.

14 A. Orley Swartzentruber, "Nouvelles de Paris," *Christ Seul*, April 1954, 9–10.

15 Orley Swartzentruber to Robert Witmer, "The Beginnings of the Work at La Butte Rouge," 21 January 2005, personal

The Creation of Mission Mennonite Française

Given these promising developments, the Swartzentrubers began to search for a permanent residence closer to the Butte-Rouge. They decided on a detached home at 10, rue Jeanne Hachette in the suburb of Clamart. Their desire to acquire property in the name of French Mennonites, with Mennonite Board of Missions and Charities funds, demonstrated the North Americans' intention to work through and with their European counterparts. As a result, Widmer later reflected, "It was natural that we made contact and that I did what was in my power to help them."[16] Initially, the parties discussed the possibility of using the Montbéliard congregation, one of the few Mennonite assemblies that was constituted as a legal association, to acquire the building. Widmer discarded this idea, considering it strange that a single congregation should hold the title for a property that would serve as a base for the common mission work of Mennonites in France. Instead, he proposed the creation of a new nonprofit legal

Mission Mennonite Française lodging for missionary family in 1954 (10 rue Jeanne Hachette, Clamart, France)

association created under the law of 1901. MBMC accepted his recommendation.[17]

Thus, Widmer and his fellow elder from the Montbéliard congregation, Pierre Sommer, established Mission Mennonite Française (MMF) in that city on October 5, 1954. The second article of MMF's founding

---

files of Robert Witmer, Cambridge, ON.

16 Pierre Widmer, "Mission Mennonite Française: Rapport Moral du Président," *Christ Seul*, November 1969, 14–16.

---

17 Ibid.

statutes laid out the association's principal goal: "Mission Mennonite Française has as its objective to make known the Word of God and the Gospel of our Savior Jesus Christ to men of our time who, in France and in the French Union, do not have the good fortune of knowing them." "To attain this objective," the third article continued, "Mission Mennonite Française proposes to open gathering places and information centers in Paris, the greater Paris area, and wherever else it may be possible to do so." The statutes stipulated that membership in the organization would require maintaining active participation and payment of a yearly fee. The association's funds would consist of these fees, monies raised through gifts, and earnings from future projects. Members would convene once a year for a general assembly, and all meetings, ordinary and extraordinary, would be announced in *Christ Seul*. A president, treasurer, and executive secretary would administer the association.[18]

Founding membership of MMF included Pierre Widmer, Pierre Sommer, Max Schowalter, René Kennel, André Kennel, and Albert Klopfenstein. These members, representing both French Mennonite conferences, were drawn to the new association because of a broad interest in missions. Many were active participants in the French Mennonite Mission Committee and hoped to see the evangelistic witness of French Mennonites grow.[19] At the association's constitutive general assembly, they entrusted the presidency of the association to Widmer, appointed Schowalter as secretary, and designated Orley Swartzentruber as executive secretary, the association's *homme à tout faire* charged with carrying out the association's work. Because of his unique dual role as MBMC missionary and only full-time worker for the French association, Swartzentruber "was specially charged with the relationship with our American friends who are interested in our work, and on whose support we count."[20] Swartzentruber's first task was to purchase the Clamart property, "in view of establishing the residence of the Mission's executive secretary there."[21]

18 Pierre Widmer, "La Mission Mennonite Française, Statuts," *Christ Seul*, January 1955, 47–48.

19 Théo Hege, e-mail message to author, 15 June 2012.

20 Minutes of the MMF General Assembly, 5 October 1954, photocopy of *Cahier Officiel* of MMF, personal files of Robert Witmer, Cambridge, ON.

21 Ibid.

The creation of MMF formalized the working arrangement that Widmer and Graber had first envisaged. MMF now served as MBMC's legal organ in France, permitting North American investments in the country to be transferred promptly into French Mennonite hands as demanded by the board's indigenization policy. The administration of MMF would remain firmly in French hands. MBMC's participation in the French association's deliberations was limited to the contributions of its own missionary, who served as MMF executive secretary.[22] By supervising, guiding, and supporting the North American representative's work, MMF promised to act as a spiritual counselor for MBMC personnel in France.[23] From MBMC's perspective, the twin functions of MMF protected the viability of North American mission work in France.[24] To ensure that channels of communication between the organizations remained open, MBMC invited the MMF president to participate in the agency's European Mission Council, a body created in September 1953 to coordinate all MBMC missionary ventures in French-speaking Europe.[25]

Foyer Fraternel, 1956-61

The Founding of a Mennonite Congregation in Châtenay-Malabry

In April 1955, Mission Mennonite Française officially transferred its office to the property in Clamart.[26] By this time, fifteen people participated regularly in Friday evening Bible study. Orley Swartzentruber continued to lead this meeting, seeking guidance in the exercise of pastoral duties both from the Shanks in Belgium and from the MMF committee in Montbéliard, but especially from André Trocmé, who had become a respected mentor.[27] Each Sunday, the Swartzentrubers rented a small bus in which they held Sunday school and

22 Wilbert Shenk, interview by David Neufeld, 25 July 2011.

23 Robert Witmer, "Domaine Emmanuel," *Christ Seul*, January 1999, 40–42.

24 Wilbert Shenk, interview by David Neufeld, 25 July 2011.

25 Harold S. Bender, "Mission Mennonite Francaise (France)" *Global Anabaptist Mennonite Encyclopedia Online*; http://www.gameo.org/encyclopedia/contents/M57834.html.

26 Minutes of the MMF General Assembly, 11 April 1955, photocopy of *Cahier Officiel* of MMF, personal files of Robert Witmer, Cambridge, ON.

27 Orley Swartzentruber to Robert Witmer, "The Beginnings of the Work at La Butte Rouge," 21 January 2005, personal files of Robert Witmer, Cambridge, ON.

Sunday morning worship and Sunday school in rented highway bus (1955). Left to right: Elisabeth Good, Andrée Deteix, Anne Sommermeyer, Roland Deteix (with back turned), Orley Swartzentruber, and Mme Rohel

worship services. After several participants asked to be baptized, a small congregation was born. J. D. Graber attended its first service, held on March 25, 1956, in the Swartzentrubers' home. Orley baptized Mmes Rohel

and Paris and accepted Anne Sommermeyer into the congregation on the transfer of her membership.[28]

In June, MMF purchased land at 249, avenue de la Division Leclerc in Châtenay-Malabry for three

Gathering for worship at Châtenay-Malabry

28 Assemblée Évangelique Mennonite du Foyer Fraternel, congregational history (1956–84) given to Robert and Lois Witmer, undated, personal files of Robert Witmer, Cambridge, ON.

Sunday school at Foyer Fraternel in Châtenay-Malabry (1957). Adults left to right: Anne Sommermeyer, M. Ondet, and Orley Swartzentruber

million francs.[29] At the rear of the property, the new congregation's members erected a grey three-by-six-meter prefabricated structure. On July 8, they inaugurated Foyer Fraternel of the Butte-Rouge. This small shed soon served as a common home for a variety of activities involving community members, including a Thursday afternoon children's club, Friday night Bible study, and Sunday morning worship services. The building also housed French classes for North Africans, Blue Cross meetings for recovering alcoholics, and the activities of La Nichée, Anne Sommermeyer's ministry to children with developmental disabilities.[30]

Robert and Lois Witmer, a Canadian missionary couple sent to Paris to cover the Swartzentrubers' first furlough, arrived soon after the congregation's birth. The Shanks and Swartzentrubers had appealed to MBMC for a third couple to join them in Europe in order to make mutual furlough replacements easier. They also hoped that an increase in personnel would allow them to respond favorably to requests for Mennonite representation at a variety of ecumenical meetings and conferences, specifically those held by Christian pacifist groups. In a time of political and social ferment, Orley explained, "a generation of theologians is discovering nonresistance and the believers' church, as if

29 Minutes of the MMF General Assembly, 9 February 1956, photocopy of *Cahier Officiel* of MMF, personal files of Robert Witmer, Cambridge, ON.

30 "Dans la Région parisienne," *Christ Seul*, August/September 1956, 16.

variety of potential directions for the future of the mission work in Paris appeared to be emerging.

However, on their arrival in Paris in November 1956, the Witmers' primary responsibility lay with the local congregation. A period of acclimatization for their young family, which included a piecemeal program of language and cultural study, did not hamper their integration into the life of the community.[33] In an installation service held during the MMF general assembly meeting at Foyer Fraternel in February 1958, Pierre Widmer charged Robert Witmer with carrying out the association's work in Châtenay-Malabry. Widmer instructed Witmer to "proclaim the Word of God to all . . . with complete faithfulness," administering the ceremonies of the church according to scriptural order; consecrating elders, deacons, and preachers; visiting church members; blessing and orienting the congregation's children, youth, and new couples; exercising discipline in a spirit of love; and calling on the support of fellow servants in the administering of the church's affairs.[34] This appointment followed MMF's designation

Robert and Lois Witmer with children settle into their home in Clamart (June 1958).

there had never been such a thing."[31] It was a North American Mennonite priority to encourage and stimulate this interest. The MBMC workers also hoped to be able to organize more frequent missionary-led weekend Bible conferences for French churches in the east of the country. Past meetings had been well received and had served as a bridge to local Mennonites.[32] A wide

---

31 Orley Swartzentruber to Robert Witmer, 22 May 1956, personal files of Robert Witmer, Cambridge, ON.
32 Ibid.

33 Robert Witmer, e-mail message to author, 14 July 2012.
34 Text of "Installation de Robert Witmer à la Butte-Rouge (Châtenay-Malabry)," 16 February 1958, personal files of

Excavation for the new Foyer Fraternel on Avenue de la Division LeClerc, Châtenay-Malabry (1958)

of Witmer as its second executive secretary.[35] Succeeding Orley Swartzentruber, he was now the principal agent responsible for advancing the association's goals. In this project, the Witmers were to receive support from André Springer, a student at the nearby Bible Institute of Nogent, who was invited to join the mission's work as an evangelist.[36]

The Swartzentrubers left France in May 1958, soon after celebrating the official opening of the site where a permanent, multistory church building was to be

Unveiling the plaque for Foyer Fraternel (May 1958). Officiating: Orley Swartzentruber (center) and Pierre Widmer (right)

Robert Witmer, Cambridge, ON.

35 Minutes of the MMF General Assembly, 23 February 1957, photocopy of *Cahier Officiel* of MMF, personal files of Robert Witmer, Cambridge, ON.

36 Minutes of the MMF General Assembly, 16 February 1958, photocopy of *Cahier Officiel* of MMF, personal files of Robert Witmer, Cambridge, ON.

Church dedication at Châtenay-Malabry (26 October 1958). Clockwise, top left to bottom left: Pierre Widmer, Montbéliard choir, Edouard Theis with André Trocmé, and Robert Witmer

constructed over a period of ten months.[37] Funded by MBMC, the structure included a sanctuary, space for meetings and classes, and a small apartment intended to lodge the missionary couple.[38] As a variety of contractors worked under the supervision of architect M. Datcharry, the congregation began an extensive publicity program, informing Protestant and evangelical churches around Paris of the new building's opening and dedication and inviting them to support the Mennonite evangelistic effort in prayer.[39] On October 26, 1958, the new Foyer Fraternel building was inaugurated in a morning worship service attended by friends from the local Reformed and Baptist churches and a dozen Mennonites from the east of France. David Shank, André Trocmé, J. D. Graber, and Pierre Widmer, each representing a source of support for the congregation, shared words of encouragement and blessed the mission's future work.[40]

Two French Mennonite volunteers and two North American MCC workers had aided in the latter stages of the construction effort, turning the church's backyard

Foyer Fraternel in Châtenay-Malabry, completed and fully functional (1959)

37 "Nouvelles de la Mission Mennonite Française," *Christ Seul*, April 1958, 6.

38 Robert Witmer and André Springer, "Chronique de l'Année 1958," *Christ Seul*, January 1959, 35–36.

39 Robert Witmer to "Dear Co-labourers in Christ," 12 November 1958, personal files of Robert Witmer, Cambridge, ON.

40 Robert Witmer and André Springer, "La Mission Mennonite Française," *Christ Seul*, January 1959, 37–38.

into a playground for community children.[41] The service of these individuals, which included renovations of the Clamart property, represented an extension of links between MCC, specifically its Pax program, and the French mission. This relationship had recently been established in Algeria and would develop over the course of the next decades.

MCC Pax and Its Early Involvement in Châtenay-Malabry

The Pax program belonged to a wave of expansion in voluntary service opportunities for young North American Mennonites after World War II.[42] The theological trends driving increased enthusiasm for overseas missions also encouraged church members, especially lay people, to practice new forms of discipleship. As historian Paul Toews explains, "servant activism and volunteerism were replacing cultural markers as the central carriers of Mennonite peoplehood. That

[postwar] generation was moving the church toward a more clearly defined theology of service and a more globally engaged missional activity."[43] Pax exemplified this movement.

The program originated in European Mennonite meetings held in 1950 that sought to address the plight of eastern European refugees temporarily housed in

Pax volunteers help finish the job of church construction at Châtenay-Malabry (September 1958). Left to right, clockwise: Ben Brubaker, Bill Babcock, Gabriel Ebersole, Alphonse Feron (from Belgium), Charlie Sauder, Ken Hochstedler, and Dale Eash

---

41 David Burkholder to Boyd Nelson, "Finishing Touches on New Paris Church," 1958, personal files of Robert Witmer, Cambridge, ON.

42 Guy F. Hershberger, *The Mennonite Church in the Second World War* (Scottdale, PA: Mennonite Publishing House, 1951), 226–31.

43 Paul Toews, *Mennonites in American Society, 1930–1970* (Scottdale, PA: Herald Press, 1996), 213.

German refugee camps. Mennonite Central Committee delegates emerged from this encounter with a desire both to construct permanent refugee housing and to provide a volunteer alternative to military service for young North American and European Mennonite conscientious objectors.[44] The urgency of the search for nonviolent avenues of service in the United States intensified after the US Congress reinstituted a military draft as a response to the outbreak of war in Korea. MCC successfully appealed to the National Service Board for Religious Objectors for an exception to the draft legislation's obstruction of foreign alternative service.[45] This provision made the Pax program a viable alternative to military service for North American youth. The MCC executive committee approved the project in December 1950.[46] MCC recruited volunteer participants through advertisements in Mennonite periodicals and encouraged churches to raise funds to subsidize the $1,800 cost of supporting the two-year assignment of each Pax volunteer.[47] After receiving two weeks of preparatory orientation at MCC headquarters in Akron, Pennsylvania, the first Pax unit arrived in Espelkamp, Nord Rhein–Westfalen, in April 1951 to begin constructing homes for refugees.

Pax, "a remarkably idealistic, naïve, flexible, experimental, and ingenious jerry-built dream," was well suited to adapt to the needs of varied circumstances.[48] Although the program grew out of the European refugee crisis, Pax was soon reconceptualized as a resource to serve many of the Mennonite community's diverse commitments to relief and service. Pax teams operated officially under the MCC executive secretary and the European Pax director, but the process of assigning them to specific projects remained structurally flexible and crossed lines of authority. MCC often lent out Pax teams to "special assignments," a designation under which Pax work for the French mission fell.[49] The Pax commitment "to promote international goodwill and understanding through the total impact of the program by working with citizens of other countries in a spirit

---

44 Calvin W. Redekop, *The Pax Story* (Telford, PA: Pandora Press U.S., 2001), 41–43.

45 Ibid., 53–55.

46 Ibid., 45.

47 Ibid., 51.

48 Ibid., 51.

49 Ibid., 76–77.

of sharing and brotherly love" resonated perfectly with the cooperative framework that shaped the developing mission effort in France.[50]

The Pax volunteers' "highly commendable job" with Foyer Fraternel's construction encouraged Witmer to pursue the possibility of a more permanent Pax presence in Paris.[51] He hoped that a Pax volunteer could free the Witmers from "non-missionary" duties like general maintenance, driving, cleaning, and entertaining guests, tasks that inhibited the missionaries from engaging more intensively in evangelistic activities.[52] Boyd Nelson, MRC secretary for relief and service, encouraged Witmer to seriously consider the "moral responsibility" of sponsoring a Pax volunteer. "If you simply want work done," he advised, "it may be easier in money, effort, and suffering to just hire the services done locally." In spite of a thorough vetting process, volunteers inevitably demonstrated "the usual problems of late adolescents and young adults." Witmer

Robert Witmer, Foyer Fraternel, Châtenay-Malabry (1958)

would need to assume responsibility for the close supervision and organization of the volunteer's activities that, besides daily tasks, would include language study and participation in the church. "But if you want to awaken some young life to the missionary call as well as get the work done cheerfully and willingly plus having the inspiration of youthful enthusiasm around, and if you are ready to put out the effort to do this,"

---

50 Ibid., 57.

51 "Pax Paris Project Report," 1 May to 16 June 1958, personal files of Robert Witmer, Cambridge, ON.

52 Robert Witmer, "??? A Pax Assignment for Paris ???," undated, personal files of Robert Witmer, Cambridge, ON.

Nelson continued, "then maybe a PAX [*sic*] man is for you."[53] Witmer consented to MCC's conditions and, soon thereafter, MBMC representatives solicited a long-term Pax volunteer for the Paris mission.[54]

The Early Life of Foyer Fraternel

Meanwhile, benefitting from a new building, the congregational life of Foyer Fraternel came to resemble that of most other French Mennonite congregations. The services and activities once housed in the church's prefabricated structure now had room to grow. Wednesday evening catechism, regular youth events, and monthly women's and members' meetings were also organized.[55] By the end of 1960, the church had nineteen baptized members, fifty-five children registered in Sunday school, and a regular attendance of fifty at Sunday morning services.[56] At the same time, Foyer Fraternel's growing confessional and cultural diversity set it apart from other French Mennonite congregations. Canadian and French Mennonites were joined in worship by local Reformed, Baptist, and Catholic believers. The congregation's heterogeneous makeup resulted from evangelism in the community but also reflected the mission's lack of success in integrating French Mennonites living in Paris into the congregation's activities.

Despite Widmer's, Witmer's, and Springer's unsuccessful attempts to deepen Foyer Fraternel's relationship with these Mennonites, other efforts were made to cultivate links with existing Mennonite groups in France. Foyer Fraternel sent invitations to MMF members and their congregations to participate in the community's evangelistic activities.[57] Continual reporting in *Christ Seul* on the partners' work in Paris built awareness and interest among church members in eastern France. Occasions including the congregation's

---

53 Boyd Nelson to Robert Witmer, 29 September 1958. Box 12, Folder 85, Mennonite Board of Missions Overseas Ministry Division Data Files Part 2, 1956–1965. IV/18/013-02. Mennonite Church USA Archives. Goshen, IN.

54 "Reports on Yoder trip to Europe and North Africa," 1959, 6, personal files of Robert Witmer, Cambridge, ON.

55 Robert Witmer to Pierre Widmer, 11 December 1958; Robert Witmer to John H. Yoder, 3 March 1960, personal files of Robert Witmer, Cambridge, ON.

56 "Mission Mennonite Française," *Christ Seul*, January 1961, 46.

57 Robert Witmer to Pierre Widmer, 20 June 1958, personal files of Robert Witmer, Cambridge, ON.

vacation Bible school offered a chance for Mennonites from this region to get to know their spiritual brothers and sisters living in the capital.[58] In addition, starting in 1959, MMF business found a place on the agenda of the French Mennonite Mission Committee, by that time a larger body connected to a greater number of Mennonite congregations.[59] As a result, its members became better acquainted with developments in Paris.

The MMF members' interest in and supervision of the missionary activity in Paris also built trust between the leadership and membership of Foyer Fraternel and French Mennonites. Pierre Widmer served as an important point of contact. Through frequent letters and visits to Paris, he offered the congregation guidance and encouragement in the development of their programs.[60] On occasion, the MMF general assembly served as a helpful sounding board for Foyer Fraternel's leadership, especially MBMC missionaries, to test ideas and receive counsel. In the search for a replacement for the Witmers during their first furlough, for instance, the assembly provided a forum for debate about the theological compatibility of potential candidates.[61] The favorable development of Foyer Fraternel's relationship with MMF resulted in the transfer of the association's office to the church property and the acceptance of the church's membership in the Conférence des assemblées Mennonites de langue française, the French-speaking Mennonite conference, at its annual meeting in St. Genis on November 13, 1960.[62]

MBMC support of the mission's activity in Châtenay-Malabry also grew. The board's confidence in its progress is evident in early discussions about a future transfer of ownership of the Foyer Fraternel building to the congregation.[63] Witmer believed that the stability of the congregation's leadership, membership, and programming warranted initiation of discussions

---

58 Robert Witmer to John H. Yoder, 3 March 1960, personal files of Robert Witmer, Cambridge, ON.

59 "Reports on Yoder trip to Europe and North Africa," 1959, 6, personal files of Robert Witmer, Cambridge, ON.

60 For example, Pierre Widmer to Robert Witmer, 22 June 1962, personal files of Robert Witmer, Cambridge, ON.

61 Minutes of the MMF General Assembly, 26 January 1961, photocopy of Cahier Officiel of MMF, personal files of Robert Witmer, Cambridge, ON.

62 Robert Witmer to John H. Yoder, 22 November 1960, personal files of Robert Witmer, Cambridge, ON.

63 Robert Witmer to John H. Yoder, 19 January 1960, personal files of Robert Witmer, Cambridge, ON.

about this step, which would eventually be mandated by board policy. John H. Yoder, now MBMC Administrative Assistant for Foreign Missions, agreed with Witmer's contention that this action would encourage a broader transfer of responsibility from the missionaries to the congregation's members. Yoder believed that the financial self-sufficiency of Foyer Fraternel would provide a good indicator of when the transfer should take place. Although this time had not yet come, Yoder encouraged Witmer to share MBMC's intentions with the congregation: "You have full authorization to go ahead yourself and say that our Board is deeply convinced of the necessity to transfer responsibility to the local congregation progressively as rapidly as the congregation is willing and able to take over."[64]

The Partners' Collaboration Extends to Algeria, 1955–71

The development of Foyer Fraternel fit within the framework to which Mission Mennonite Française and Mennonite Board of Missions and Charities had committed themselves and so served to strengthen the organizations' trust in each other. A joint project in Algeria, then an overseas territory of France, built further confidence in their partnership. In 1955, MBMC had initiated and funded a program of reconstruction, relief, and mission in Orléansville, Algeria, in response to an earthquake. This action was carried out under the legal sponsorship of MMF. The French association had designated John H. Yoder as the project's director of volunteers.[65] He oversaw the arrival of a team of Pax volunteers that provided labor for the construction of a new village for local residents. Over the next several years, this "discreet" but "powerful witness to the love of Christ" grew.[66] MBMC sent workers Carol and Miller Stayrook and Lila Rae and Robert Stetter to oversee the completion of the construction project and to maintain positive relationships with local authorities and other missions working in increasingly precarious political conditions. Annie Haldemann, a nurse, was sent to Algiers in 1958 to begin Arabic study and literacy training with a long-term assignment to staff

64 John H. Yoder to Robert Witmer, 26 January 1960, personal files of Robert Witmer, Cambridge, ON.

65 Minutes of the MMF General Assembly, 11 April 1955, photocopy of the *Cahier Officiel* of the MMF, personal files of Robert Witmer, Cambridge, ON.

66 "Nouvelles de la Mission Mennonite Française," *Christ Seul*, April 1958, 6–7.

a community center that would serve as a home base for missionary work in the city.[67] Yoder, Widmer, and Witmer made frequent trips to Algeria to assess the project's progress.[68]

In early 1959, MBMC proposed a complete handover of the Algerian mission's direction to MMF while maintaining full funding for the project.[69] The April meetings of the European Mission Council halted serious consideration of this proposal. The council recommended the decentralization of field responsibility for each of the MBMC missionary efforts in French-speaking Europe. This decision responded to doubts about the council's effectiveness in articulating a broader missionary strategy for the projects it incorporated. It meant that "major responsibility [was] distributed both downward to the several field committees and upward to the Elkhart office [MBMC headquarters]."[70] Several consequences of this development were clear. The intensity of interaction and coordination between MBMC missionaries in Europe would diminish, and a measure of administrative authority would move out of the field back to North America.[71] In Algeria, this decision appeared to diminish the possibility for increased French responsibility for the project initiated by North Americans. Until 1971 MMF continued to provide legal representation for the Algerian work, which came to include payment of benefits to missionary personnel while they were on furlough in France.[72] However, MBMC personnel on site or in the United States would make all important administrative decisions. In metropolitan France, however, the diminished decision-mak-

---

67 Minutes of the MMF General Assembly, 27 March 1959, photocopy of *Cahier Officiel* of MMF, personal files of Robert Witmer, Cambridge, ON.

68 Annie Haldemann, "La MMF en Algerie pendant l'Année 1959," *Christ Seul*, January 1960, 53–54.

69 Minutes of the MMF General Assembly, 27 March 1959, photocopy of *Cahier Officiel* of MMF, personal files of Robert Witmer, Cambridge, ON.

70 "Reports on Yoder trip to Europe and North Africa," 1959, 2, personal files of Robert Witmer, Cambridge, ON.

71 Letter from John H. Yoder to David Shank, 2 March 1961, personal files of Robert Witmer, Cambridge, ON.

72 Minutes of the MMF General Assembly, 5 February 1966 and 11 November 1971, photocopy of *Cahier Officiel* of MMF, personal files of Robert Witmer, Cambridge, ON. MMF's official legal status enabled the association to provide this function also for French Mennonite Mission Committee missionaries on furlough from Chad, Indonesia, and New Caledonia.

ing role of the council demanded a more engaged stance from MMF. Growing out of a "more or less formal" role, MMF would have to shoulder a heavier responsibility for substantive policy decisions.[73] The surrender to MMF of MBMC administrative control over its personnel and programming in France had been agreed on from the beginning of the agencies' relationship. The council's determination reinforced this arrangement.

A Ministry for Youth with Developmental Disabilities: Les Amis de l'Atelier, 1957–64

Anne Sommermeyer Works with Children with Developmental Disabilities

In Châtenay-Malabry, the development of Foyer Fraternel over the next years was shaped by the creation and growth of a project serving youth with developmental disabilities, which originated in Anne Sommermeyer's ministry at La Nichée. Sommermeyer's work with children began during her time as a kindergarten tutor in Paris before the war. An encounter with a six-year-old boy with developmental disabilities inspired "love at first sight, a feeling that would orient a

Anne Sommermeyer offered educational classes at La Nichée beginning in early 1957.

whole life toward service to the mentally handicapped," a life lived in protest against a world that viewed human beings as expendable.[74] After the war, Sommermeyer pursued her passion by educating a small group of children with disabilities in her small apartment in Châtenay-Malabry. Her service, offered on a voluntary basis, addressed a pressing need. Most of the hundreds of thousands of people with mental disorders in France

---

73 "Reports on Yoder trip to Europe and North Africa," 1959, 6, personal files of Robert Witmer, Cambridge, ON.

74 Sommermeyer, "Un itinéraire," 842.

did not receive proper care.[75] The French government had declared mental disability a "long sickness" and refused to reimburse drug costs after two years of coverage.[76] The strain that these institutional failures placed on Sommermeyer's work was compounded by intolerance toward her efforts shown by neighbors in her own building. Foyer Fraternel's prefabricated building provided an alternate home for La Nichée starting in early 1957. Throughout the week Sommermeyer now offered educational classes for children and adolescents with developmental disabilities. She hoped to help her pupils overcome their difficulties by creating an atmosphere of faith and love and by providing a space for them to form enriching social ties outside their homes. In her contact with pupils' parents, Sommermeyer saw an opportunity for outreach.[77] As a result, Witmer acknowledged, "the school for retarded children is progressively becoming a part of the witness of the local church."[78]

The teenagers in the group provided La Nichée's director with a unique challenge. Unable to attend school or hold down a job, these youth represented a heavy burden for their families. As a consequence, many parents abandoned their children to the state. Sommermeyer developed an artisanal solution to this dilemma. She created a small sheltered workshop where the young men as part of a group carried out tasks adapted to their abilities. The simple manufactured products they assembled were sold in the community, and the profits were reinvested in materials and given to the workers as pocket money.[79] Initially, this arrangement proved to be unsustainable. Products did not sell, parents were unable or unwilling to subsidize the cost of the workshop, and Sommermeyer was left exhausted.[80]

---

75 Anne Sommermeyer, "Servir au nom de Christ," *Christ Seul*, November 1961, 10–11.

76 Sommermeyer, "Un itinéraire," 845.

77 Anne Sommermeyer, "Au Service de l'Enfance et de l'Adolescence Déficients," *Christ Seul*, April 1958, 7–8.

78 Robert Witmer, "Growing Pains," January 1959, personal files of Robert Witmer, Cambridge, ON.

79 Anne Sommermeyer, "Au Service de l'Enfance et de l'Adolescence Déficients," *Christ Seul*, April 1958, 7–8.

80 Sommermeyer, "Un itinéraire," 847.

Foyer Fraternel Gets Involved and Founds Les Amis de l'Atelier

In the wake of the workshop's failure, in 1961 Foyer Fraternel's members launched a coordinated effort to help youth with developmental disabilities. Based closely on Sommermeyer's original model, this new project sought to establish a center for older participants of La Nichée and eligible youth from the community. In addition to expanding the size of Sommermeyer's effort, this undertaking differed from its predecessor in its funding structure. In the spring of 1961, Sommermeyer and Witmer made contact with representatives from the Social Welfare Department who expressed an interest in the creation of a *centre d'aide par le travail*, a sheltered workshop for people with developmental disabilities, in Châtenay-Malabry.[81] The officials informed them that the department could provide funding to an accredited workshop in the form of a *prix de journée*, a per diem rate paid for each worker, intended to defray the costs of the workshop's operating budget. Public funding promised long-term financial viability.

Up to this point, neither MBMC nor any French Mennonite entity had attempted to seek state subsidies to support their projects.[82]

The congregation and MMF received the idea of a state-funded but church-sponsored venture with some hesitation.[83] How would the program's operation and funds be administered? Who would staff the center? What pressures would the project place on available space? What impact would the program have on the congregation's existing ministries and its witness to the gospel? The approval of all local parties, on which MBMC support hinged, depended on the project organizers' assurances that the work would retain an evangelistic quality and that its development would, in all circumstances, remain under the direction and administration of the church and MMF. In a meeting of the MMF general assembly, Sommermeyer persuaded the association's members of the spiritual nature of service to youth with developmental disabilities. "It is a

---

81 Pamphlet, Victor Hugo Dos Santos, "Association des Établissements du Domaine Emmanuel: 2004, 50 Ans Déjà . . .," 2004, 7.

82 Wilbert Shenk, interview by David Neufeld, 1 June 2012.

83 Robert Witmer, "A Propos du Centre Médico-Pédagogique du Foyer Fraternel, Châtenay-Malabry," May 1964, personal files of Robert Witmer, Cambridge, ON.

The sheltered workshop met in the church basement at Châtenay-Malabry beginning in September 1961.

testimony," she argued. "I am above all a missionary."[84] In order to guarantee the church's ongoing witness to the project and its participants, it was decided that a new association, Les Amis de l'Atelier (Friends of the Workshop), would be founded, composed exclusively of Foyer Fraternel members. Its board, led by church member Roger Kennel, would be charged with direc-

tion and administration of the new project. Since Foyer Fraternel functioned under the supervision of MMF, links between the association and the workshop's leadership would be established automatically.[85] Convinced of the project's potential, MMF, MBMC, and the Foyer Fraternel membership authorized their representatives to proceed. Provisionally, the church building's basement would provide a testing ground for the project, allowing it to function but limiting the participating parties' initial commitment in case they considered a continuation of the work undesirable.[86]

The workshop's opening was complicated by a Social Welfare Department policy that demanded that the project begin functioning before it received accreditation and became eligible for public funding.[87] Because of a lack of local start-up funds, MBMC agreed to advance money to Les Amis de l'Atelier; this money was later

84 Minutes of the MMF General Assembly, 17 February 1962, photocopy of *Cahier Officiel* of MMF, personal files of Robert Witmer, Cambridge, ON.

85 Robert Witmer, "A Propos du Centre Médico-Pédagogique du Foyer Fraternel, Châtenay-Malabry," May 1964, personal files of Robert Witmer, Cambridge, ON.

86 Robert Witmer to John H. Yoder, 16 May 1962, personal files of Robert Witmer, Cambridge, ON.

87 Robert Witmer, e-mail message to author, 5 October 2012.

refunded by the state.[88] As a result, the congregation was able to arrange and furnish its basement to conform to official specifications. After the department's inspector approved the center's capacity to achieve its objectives, Witmer negotiated a prix de journée of 5,50 francs per worker per day.[89] With these funds, the association drafted a budget to cover the salary of Anne Sommermeyer's husband, Hans, who was hired as the workshop's manager. On September 15, 1961, Foyer Fraternel opened a workshop that offered adapted work to twelve young men and women with disabilities.[90] The center was among the first sheltered workshops in France.

The Early Life of Les Amis de l'Atelier

From this date forward, the Centre d'aide par le travail operated forty hours a week in the church's basement. Workers acted as subcontractors for businesses, assembling electronics or handling small goods. They were remunerated according to their production and received social security benefits.[91] The workshop was managed by Hans Sommermeyer, with the help of several volunteers. Anne Sommermeyer played the principal administrative role in the center's everyday functioning while continuing to direct La Nichée.

It became clear that the workshop needed a larger staff. In Christ Seul, Anne Sommermeyer issued "an urgent call to all of our youth," asking them to sacrifice their own comforts to work with the least fortunate. Service in Paris offered opportunity for spiritual development, practical training, and participation in a new congregation, she explained. Young people not ready to take this step could support others financially.[92] Sommermeyer's request for help did not immediately draw large numbers of Mennonite volunteers from eastern France to Paris. However, a renegotiation of the prix de journée to cover utility expenses and permit "normal remuneration" of all workers went some distance in addressing temporary staffing shortages.[93]

---

88 Ibid.; and John H. Yoder to Robert Witmer, 23 June 1961, personal files of Robert Witmer, Cambridge, ON.

89 Robert Witmer, interview by David Neufeld, 7 June 2012.

90 Anne Sommermeyer, "Servir au nom de Christ," Christ Seul, November 1961, 10–11.

91 Sommermeyer, "Un itinéraire," 848.

92 Anne Sommermeyer, "Servir au nom de Christ," Christ Seul, November 1961, 10–11.

93 Letter from Robert Witmer to John H. Yoder, J. D. Graber, H. Ernest Bennett, 2 November 1962, personal files of Robert

The decision to install the workshop in the church basement had clearly been provisional, and Les Amis de l'Atelier soon looked to establish a permanent location for the Centre d'aide par le travail. In October 1962, neighbor Mme Gaillard put a 350-square-meter parcel of property that lay adjacent to Foyer Fraternel up for sale, and the association immediately considered its purchase.[94] The workshop's leadership hoped to construct a space that would house the center for youth and La Nichée, opening the possibility for a more "closely coordinated project."[95] When approached with these plans, MMF representatives soon abandoned the idea of a four-story inclusive facility on the lot. Rather, they approved the construction of a *préau fermée*, a ground-level structure, intended solely to house the workshop's activities.[96] However, some remained skeptical about MMF's capacity to raise the funds necessary to cover the capital expenses.

Aware that the Social Welfare Department would subsidize building costs gradually through its prix de journée, Witmer contacted MBMC leadership on behalf of MMF, requesting a loan from the board's property investment fund.[97] John H. Yoder's negative response to this request, based on budgetary constraints, was accompanied by a number of questions that tested the plans for the workshop's expansion. Yoder asked Witmer whether the congregation's members and the workshop's staff were ready for the obligations inherent in an expansion into real estate. He shared concerns about the "evangelistic effectiveness" of the project, although the work with youth with disabilities had created positive relationships between the church and the community. "Might the community good will, as has so often been the case in other missionary institutions, be of such a kind as not to contribute markedly to church growth?" he wondered. Yoder encouraged Witmer to carefully evaluate the commitment of MMF and

Witmer, Cambridge, ON.

94 Robert Witmer to John H. Yoder, 17 October 1962, personal files of Robert Witmer, Cambridge, ON.

95 Letter from Robert Witmer to John H. Yoder, J. D. Graber, H. Ernest Bennett, 2 November 1962, personal files of Robert Witmer, Cambridge, ON.

96 Robert Witmer, e-mail message to author, 5 October 2012.

97 Letter from Robert Witmer to John H. Yoder, J. D. Graber, H. Ernest Bennett, 2 November 1962, personal files of Robert Witmer, Cambridge, ON.

the local congregation to the project and its proposed expansion.[98]

In his response, Witmer acknowledged that these questions had not been absent from the minds of the workshop's leadership.[99] Indeed, while it had initially been the congregation's concern that the expansion of the workshop not hinder the growth of the church's other activities and ministries, the heavy demands placed on the church leadership's time and energy by the Centre d'aide par le travail caused these fears to re-emerge. Steps taken to initiate the workshop's expansion preceded thorough discernment over the future development of the project. This circumstance contributed to development of tensions between the center's supervising association, its directors, and MBMC missionaries.[100]

In these circumstances, Pierre Widmer, representing MMF, played an important role as mediator.

Through frequent correspondence and visits, he and the rest of the association's general assembly became well acquainted with the strains the Centre d'aide par le travail was placing on the young congregation. As a body, they saw a need for greater engagement in the Paris mission on the part of French Mennonites. While the work in Châtenay-Malabry had been launched by North Americans, Les Amis de l'Atelier was formed at the initiative of an indigenous congregation, and in the future the financing and personnel for the center would have to be almost exclusively French. "Are French Mennonites ready to assume responsibility for it?" they asked themselves.[101]

These early discussions involving MMF, MBMC, and Foyer Fraternel's decision-making bodies raised important questions about the workshop's direction that continued to challenge the project as it developed. Yet, despite ongoing difficulties, the congregation was convinced that the workshop remained a powerful witness to the gospel in their community.[102]

98 John H. Yoder to Robert Witmer, 8 November 1962, personal files of Robert Witmer, Cambridge, ON.

99 Robert Witmer to John H. Yoder, 3 January 1963, personal files of Robert Witmer, Cambridge, ON.

100 Robert Witmer to members of Foyer Fraternel, 18 January and 21 May 1963, personal files of Robert Witmer, Cambridge, ON.

101 Minutes of the MMF General Assembly, 7 March 1963, photocopy of *Cahier Officiel* of MMF, personal files of Robert Witmer, Cambridge, ON.

102 "Châtenay-Malabry," *Christ Seul*, February 1963, 12–13.

Making use of André Kennel's equipment from Hautefeuille to dig the foundation for the expanded sheltered workshop in October 1963

The plans for expansion eventually received support from an unexpected source. In 1963, Anne Sommermeyer's friend Mme Devic was diagnosed with terminal cancer. This illness forced her to place her son Michel, who had developmental disabilities, in a home in southern France. While in hospital, Mme Devic gladly received pastoral care from the Witmers and began to read the New Testament, a process through which she found peace with God. This spiritual awakening and

Mme Devic's concern for her son's well-being led her to offer to will her inheritance to MMF. Mme Devic proposed that in return for their assuming long-term responsibility for Michel, she would give the association her assets to be used for the extension of the partners' mission. MMF agreed to honor this request.[103] One week later, after reading the story of Ananias and Sapphira in Acts 5, Mme Devic called the Witmers to ask for forgiveness, informing them that the sum she would commit to the association was in fact almost five times what she had initially offered.[104]

Mme Devic's generosity allowed MMF to purchase Mme Gaillard's lot in 1963 and covered the cost of much of the required building supplies. Jacques Bredèche, a local building contractor, encouraged his suppliers to sell materials to MMF at reduced prices, and Alfred Grauer, a sawmill owner and operator from

103 Minutes of the MMF General Assembly, 24 November 1962, photocopy of *Cahier Officiel* of MMF, personal files of Robert Witmer, Cambridge, ON.

104 Robert Witmer, "Life in the Face of Death," 1963, personal files of Robert Witmer, Cambridge, ON; Robert Witmer to John Howard Yoder, 3 January 1963, personal files of Robert Witmer, Cambridge, ON; and Robert Witmer, e-mail message to author, 5 October 2012.

Construction under way

Alsace, donated the lumber required for the construction of the préau roof.[105] In October 1963, Gilbert Klopfenstein and three Pax volunteers joined local specialists to construct the facility.[106] On March 1, 1964, the Foyer Fraternel members dedicated the new building, which more than doubled the workshop's capacity.[107] This structure did not prohibit construction of a larger

building in the future, but it would serve the Centre d'aide par le travail indefinitely, if existing plans were to change.[108]

Unfortunately, the installation of the workshop in its new home coincided with the departure of the Sommermeyers from both Foyer Fraternel and its ministry to youth with developmental disabilities. Conflict between Anne Sommermeyer and church representatives, including the congregation's council and the Witmers, had led to a distancing of the church's leadership from the everyday functioning of the Centre d'aide par le travail. This dynamic threatened the congregation's spiritual direction of the project. Tensions threatened to paralyze "the Church's entire life" and transform the workshop from an expression of the congregation's faith into "a poor testimony for outsiders."[109] For the Foyer Fraternel council, this situation was unacceptable. In April, it concluded that "the work accomplished among the mentally handicapped is no longer

---

105 Robert Witmer, e-mail message to author, 5 October 2012.

106 "Au foyer fraternel de Châtenay-Malabry," *Christ Seul*, November 1963, 16.

107 "Châtenay-Malabry," *Christ Seul*, January 1965, 18–20.

108 Robert Witmer to John H. Yoder, 3 January 1963, personal files of Robert Witmer, Cambridge, ON.

109 Steering committee of "Les Amis de l'Atelier" to Anne Sommermeyer, April 1964, personal files of Robert Witmer, Cambridge, ON.

Hans Sommermeyer with workers in newly completed workshop, dedicated March 1, 1964

carried out in the missionary spirit of the Church."[110] Recognizing Anne Sommermeyer's great pedagogical gifts, the congregation's representatives invited her to stay on as primary educator for La Nichée, while relieving her of all administrative duties of the workshop. She declined this offer. One month later, at a meeting attended by representatives of the church's council, the leadership of Les Amis de l'Atelier, and MMF ad-

ministrators Max Schowalter and Pierre Widmer, the Sommermeyers resigned from their positions in the workshop with the assurance that they would receive support from those gathered as they explored new opportunities for service.[111] It was decided that Foyer Fraternel, through Les Amis de l'Atelier, would retain responsibility for the workshop. The Sommermeyers would create a new association for La Nichée, organize its transfer to a new location, and take responsibility for its growth and development.[112]

While this process permitted a restoration of the congregation's spiritual direction of the workshop's activities, the prospect of the Sommermeyers' absence generated uncertainty about the center's future, given the vital role the couple had played in its development and functioning.[113] A way forward emerged when Robert Witmer agreed to serve as the workshop's inter-

110 Ibid.

111 Minutes of meeting of Les Amis de l'Atelier steering committee, council of Foyer Fraternel, MMF representative, and Sommermeyers, 2 May 1964, personal files of Robert Witmer, Cambridge, ON.

112 Minutes of meeting of members of Foyer Fraternel and Sommermeyers, 24 May 1964, personal files of Robert Witmer, Cambridge, ON.

113 Robert Witmer, e-mail message to author, 5 October 2012.

im administrative director and Hans Sommermeyer committed to stay on as workshop manager until the new Nichée opened in January 1965.[114] Witmer reassigned his director's salary to pay administrative assistant M. Davillerd, whose diligent work helped free the MMF executive secretary to dedicate himself with several pivotal developments that would shape MMF and MBMC joint work in the Paris region for the next decades.

The Partners Support Work with Youth with Developmental Disabilities, 1964–67

New Opportunities for Work with Youth with Disabilities Emerge

Witmer's attention was directed in part toward an opportunity to expand the mission's work with youth with developmental disabilities; it emerged in the village of Hautefeuille, located fifty kilometers east of Paris. Beginning in 1958, Foyer Fraternel had organized church retreats at the Hautefeuille home of

The half-basement at Foyer Fraternel served multiple functions for youth group and other church activities.

MMF general assembly member André Kennel and his wife, Lilianne.[115] Their land, which surrounded a twenty-two-room château, had once served as a hunting getaway for wealthy Parisians. The Kennels' decision to sell in 1964 occasioned discussions between the couple and Witmer about the possible creation of

114 Michel Paret, "L'Action Sociale Mennonite en France au XX° Siècle: Approches Diachronique et Analytique" (PhD diss., École Pratique des Hautes Études, Sorbonne, Paris, 1997), 264.

115 Robert Witmer, "Domaine Emmanuel," *Christ Seul*, January 1999, 40–42.

Les Amis de l'Atelier reached full capacity with forty-eight youth in 1964.

a rural sheltered workshop with boarding facilities on the Hautefeuille property.[116]

MBMC had not initially foreseen the creation of social ministries by its missionaries in Paris. Yet, given the positive growth of the workshop in Châtenay-Malabry, the board supported these exploratory discussions. "The social need for this kind of service, the appropriateness of this service as a mode of witness, the possibility of getting financial resources to keep it going once undertaken, the value of such a center at Hautefeuille, and the specific adequacy of the 'formule' which you have made work in Châtenay I think are all clearly established," Yoder wrote to Witmer.[117] MBMC's central concern remained the level of local support for the program among French Mennonites, especially in the form of technically and spiritually qualified personnel. "It is the point to which we would need to trust the judgment of the French brethren," Yoder concluded.[118]

MMF representatives would come to share MBMC's concerns about personnel as the French association's purchase of the Hautefeuille property became a more concrete possibility in the summer of 1966.[119] However, in early 1965, discussions between the Kennels and MMF leadership were put on hold as the latter group's attentions were redirected toward a potential expansion of the Les Amis de l'Atelier workshop in Châtenay-Malabry.

In response to the rapid growth of the number of families requesting space in the sheltered workshop for their youth with developmental disabilities, Les Amis de l'Atelier had created a facility for a group of twelve workers in their prefabricated structure soon after Anne Sommermeyer's departure in the summer of 1964. Shortly thereafter, MMF purchased an old trolley bus from the Régie Autonome des Transports de Paris (RATP), the city's transportation authority, as a work space for twelve more workers, stretching Les Amis de l'Atelier's capacity to forty-eight youth.[120]

---

116 Robert Witmer, "Un Rêve Réaliste," *Christ Seul*, May 1981, xviii–xix.

117 John H. Yoder to Robert Witmer, 15 December 1964, personal files of Robert Witmer, Cambridge, ON.

118 Ibid.

---

119 Pierre Widmer to Robert Witmer, 5 August 1966, personal files of Robert Witmer, Cambridge, ON.

120 Robert Witmer, "Une porte ouverte à Châtenay-Malabry," *Christ Seul*, July 1966, 19–20.

Now, neighbors M. Rebiffé and his sister, owners of a 2900-square-meter property adjacent to the workshop's new préau fermé, had decided to sell their lot. Immediately, members of MMF, MBMC, and Foyer Fraternal embarked on an intense period of discernment as they formulated an appropriate response to this opportunity.

In exploratory conversations with a high-ranking representative of the Direction de la Population et de l'Action Sociale, the government body that supervised independent state-funded social projects, Witmer learned that French authorities were prioritizing creation of residences and sheltered workshops for people with developmental disorders in their upcoming *cinquième plan*, a government budgeting framework that determined spending over the five-year period from 1966 to 1970.[121] Robert Guth and Gérard Peterschmitt, two young administrators of French Mennonite background who served as regional directors in the Social Welfare Department, confirmed this information. They had become acquainted with the Foyer Fraternel workshop, an "extremely worthwhile accomplishment" in Guth's estimation, and had met with Witmer to express their support for a potential expansion of its operations through the purchase of the Rebiffé property.[122] In a letter to his brother-in-law, John H. Yoder, Guth reiterated these feelings: "I think that this is a great opportunity for witness in action, a solid base for evangelization, and an excellent possibility to involve young French Mennonites who will simultaneously find a profession in Christian service."[123] Guth believed that state subsidies for an expansion of the existing Centre d'aide par le travail would be readily available in the future, and offered to join Peterschmitt in facilitating any necessary administrative processes.

MMF Codifies a Broadening of Its Missionary Program

As a response to a potential expansion of its work in Châtenay-Malabry with youth with developmental disabilities, MMF decided to modify its statutes in an extraordinary meeting of its general assembly on May 1, 1965. In addition to its principal goal "to make known the Word of God and the Gospel of our Savior Jesus Christ to men of our time," the association

---

121 Robert Witmer to John H. Yoder, 25 February 1965, personal files of Robert Witmer, Cambridge, ON.

122 Memorandum, John H. Yoder to J. D. Graber, 12 May 1965, personal files of Robert Witmer, Cambridge, ON.

123 Ibid.

now committed also "to serve humanity in the name of Christ without distinction of race or religion, especially youth and the disadvantaged, according to their needs." This commitment, MMF members recognized, would require the opening of "residential centers and centers for mutual aid." The association's fifth article now officially authorized acceptance of government subsidies as a legitimate source of funding. As a non-profit association, MMF "decided unanimously to re-invest all future profits in its work with a view toward improving its service."[124]

The first priority of MMF remained evangelism. However, with these alterations to its founding document, the association codified its desire to advance a comprehensive missionary program that included service to spiritual and social needs, a program it had pursued in practice since Les Amis de l'Atelier had opened its sheltered workshop in 1961. Among French Mennonites, there existed an increasing awareness of and interest in the type of work in which the association was engaging. This attitude was shaped by the community's experience with the Mont des Oiseaux children's home, which had cared for children with developmental disabilities beginning in the late 1950s.[125] Like the workshop of Les Amis de l'Atelier, it received state subsidies to support its efforts. Mennonites came to associate these two projects with each other, raising the Paris project's profile. But this development also meant that questions about the missionary effectiveness of the children's home were also applied to MMF work around Paris. Some wondered what place conversion, baptism, and evangelism would have in these projects.[126]

Despite these hesitations, or perhaps because of them, MMF decided to open its membership to all members of French Mennonite congregations, for the purpose of encouraging a greater sense of ownership in the association's work. Appeals were made through *Christ Seul*,[127] and within a year Witmer reported in the

124 Minutes of extraordinary meeting of the MMF General Assembly, 1 May 1965, photocopy of *Cahier Officiel* of MMF, personal files of Robert Witmer, Cambridge, ON.

125 Théo Hege, *Le Mont des Oiseaux: Histoire d'une Oeuvre Associative et Caritative*, Les Dossiers de Christ Seul 2–3 (Montbéliard: Éditions Mennonites, 2002), 57.

126 Théo Hege, e-mail message to author, 15 June 2012.

127 For example Pierre Widmer, "Qui veut participer à la Mission Mennonite Française?" *Christ Seul*, December 1965.

periodical that more than 120 individuals representing every French Mennonite congregation from both conferences had requested membership in MMF.[128] The association's annual general assembly would retain its role as the body providing general spiritual and administrative direction to MMF work, while a newly created executive council was tasked with overseeing everyday operations of MMF ministries. This body, composed of MMF founding members and its executive secretary, invited Robert Guth, Gérard Peterschmitt, and several businessmen to join it as members to provide "informed counsel and support."[129]

To further encourage French Mennonite commitment to MMF work, and to raise funds for the potential expansion of the workshop, the association developed a mechanism to elicit their financial support. Service Épargne Mennonite (SEM; Mennonite Savings Service) was the brainchild of Witmer who, in keeping with his entrepreneurial spirit, continued to demonstrate resourcefulness in generating funds for the development of MMF programs.[130] SEM soon began functioning as a central loan fund, offering contributors interest rates comparable to those of other mutual savings banks.[131]

Expansion of the Les Amis de l'Atelier Workshop

In view of these positive steps, the MMF general assembly decided unanimously to purchase the Rebiffé lot in July 1965.[132] The French association's decision demonstrated its confidence that French Mennonites would support the type of social work that MMF continued to pursue. This determination also reflected the trust that MMF had built with their North American collaborators. The partners maintained a shared outlook, reflecting a common faith in the missionary call. MBMC had respected its fundamental commitment to work through MMF and to yield administrative control of its mission work to the association, and the efforts of

128 Robert Witmer, "Une porte ouverte à Châtenay-Malabry," *Christ Seul*, July 1966, 19–20.

129 Robert Witmer, "A Summary Photographical Sketch of MBM/MCC and MMF Partnership in Mission and Service, Châtenay-Malabry, 1954 to 1974" (presentation, Fairview Mennonite Home, Cambridge, ON, 31 October 2010).

130 Wilbert Shenk, interview by David Neufeld, 25 July 2011.

131 Pierre Sommer, "Mission Mennonite Française," *Christ Seul*, July 1980, 14.

132 Minutes of the MMF General Assembly, 2 July 1965, photocopy of *Cahier Officiel* of MMF, personal files of Robert Witmer, Cambridge, ON.

Special meeting of Mission Mennonite Française where decision is made to expand facilities. Left to right: Pierre Sommer, Robert Witmer, Pierre Widmer, René Kennel, André Kennel, Albert Klopfenstein, and Max Schowalter

association executive secretary Robert Witmer to act as the partners' primary go-between had facilitated fruitful collaboration.[133] The North American organization demonstrated its support for MMF purchase of the

Rebiffé lot by providing their counterparts with a sizeable loan. These funds supplemented a larger loan obtained by the French association from Caisse d'Épargne by mortgaging Foyer Fraternel, an MMF property.[134]

On behalf of MMF, city architect M. Fontaine began to draw up plans for a two-story building with a

The adjacent Rebiffé orchard lot, available for purchase (1965)

133 Pierre Widmer, "Qui veut participer à la Mission Mennonite Française?" *Christ Seul*, December 1965.

134 Minutes of the MMF General Assembly, 2 July 1965, photocopy of *Cahier Officiel* of MMF, personal files of Robert Witmer, Cambridge, ON; and Robert Witmer, e-mail message to author, 5 October 2012.

large workshop and staff apartments to be erected on the property. A team of five Pax volunteers, posted on special assignment in Châtenay-Malabry by MCC, began construction on the site in March 1966 following a ground-breaking ceremony led by MMF president Pierre Widmer.[135] They were later joined by Foyer Fraternel member André Gaudillère.[136] MCC's initial decision to charge the Paris mission with the volunteers' maintenance fees had been contested by Witmer, who believed the workshop's ministry "vividly expresse[d] both the 'mission' and 'service' witness of the 'one church' we represent."[137] To the project's great benefit, MCC's position was soon reversed by Peter Dyck, who assured MMF representatives that MCC would assume full financial responsibility for their volunteers.[138]

The cost of the project, which the Pax volunteers' labor had already dramatically reduced, was further subsidized by donations and loans from French Mennonites, which were channeled through SEM, and

Pierre Widmer, Mission Mennonite Française president, turning the first sod (spring 1966). Others left to right: André Gaudillère, three Pax volunteers (Gary Nafziger, Daniel Bontrager, and Harold Groff), Jacques Hergott, André Kennel, Théo Hege, M. Fontaine (architect), and Allen Richer

135 Théo Hege, "Châtenay-Malabry," *Christ Seul*, May 1966, 12–13.

136 Robert Witmer, "Une porte ouverte à Châtenay-Malabry," *Christ Seul*, July 1966, 19–20.

137 Robert Witmer to Wilbert Shenk, 11 January 1966, personal files of Robert Witmer, Cambridge, ON.

138 Robert Witmer to Peter Dyck, 14 February 1966. Box 2, Folder 86. Mennonite Board of Missions Overseas Ministry

Division Data Files Part 3, 1966–1969. IV/18/013-03. Mennonite Church USA Archives. Goshen, IN.

Construction completed (1967)

which permitted the purchase of building materials. The dedication of the workshop's new building was formally celebrated in a Sunday morning service of Foyer Fraternel on November 12, 1967.[139] With this new facility, Les Amis de l'Atelier finally had adequate permanent space for its forty-eight workers. The directorship of the workshop was now held by Théo Hege, who had arrived in Paris in September 1965 after his completion of specialized studies in social work. Les Amis de l'Atelier had appointed Hege on the recommendation of MMF, which had seen him as a technically qualified and spiritually prepared replacement for interim director Robert Witmer.[140]

The creation and development of the workshop and its sponsoring congregation were accomplished with some difficulty. Institutional and personal relationships had been tested, sometimes to the breaking point. Yet after a decade, the fruits of the partnership between North American and European Mennonites were evident. Foyer Fraternel was a growing congregation offering a diverse and comprehensive Christian witness unique among Protestant and evangelical missions in France.[141] After a brief visit to Paris, Widmer reflected on the outcomes of the partners' joint efforts. Workers of the Centre d'aide par le travail carried out their labor "in a morally healthy milieu, where an atmosphere of

139 Pierre Widmer, "L'Ouverture et la Dédicace du Domaine Emmanuel," *Christ Seul*, January 1968, 15–18.

140 Minutes of the MMF General Assembly, 16 January 1965, photocopy of *Cahier Officiel* of MMF, personal files of Robert Witmer, Cambridge, ON.

141 Allen V. Koop, *American Evangelical Missionaries in France 1945–1975* (Lanham, MD: University Press of America, 1986), 91.

kindness and love, the witness of God's Word, and the liberating message of the Gospel of our Savior Jesus Christ prevail." Nearly sixty adults and thirty children attended Sunday morning worship services, and youth played an increasing role in the life of the church. "What strikes the visitor the most," Widmer enthused, "is the life that reigns at Foyer Fraternel; one almost wants to write the life that teems."[142]

---

142 Pierre Widmer, "Chronique du Foyer Fraternel," *Christ Seul*, January 1964, 32.

3
"To Serve in the Name of Christ"
Partnership Strengthens and Matures, 1966–84

In 1967, Mennonite Board of Missions and Charities and Eastern Mennonite Board of Missions and Charities convened a European Mission Study Conference in Basel, Switzerland, to which they invited representatives of their European partner agencies, a variety of North American Mennonite mission boards, and Mennonite Central Committee. Although several local delegates challenged the North American evaluation of Europe as an opportune mission field, Mission Mennonite Française representative Pierre Widmer supported this assessment wholeheartedly.[1] A desire to respond to these circumstances, shared by French and North American Mennonites, had inspired the formation of a partnership in mission between MMF and MBMC, at times in collaboration with MCC, that had yielded significant fruits. As the partners moved forward together, they continued to explore how to shape a faithful witness that addressed the needs their missionaries encountered. This process of discovery and discernment led to a diversification of approaches and strategies, each of which shaped the relationship between the organizations over the next twenty years.

Domaine Emmanuel at Hautefeuille, 1966–73

Plans for a Rural Centre d'aide par le travail for Youth with Developmental Disabilities
In the latter half of the 1960s, the partners' efforts increasingly revolved around the development of a rural sheltered workshop and residence on the estate of André and Lilianne Kennel in Hautefeuille for youth with developmental disabilities. The Kennels had given MMF purchase priority for the property in 1964 soon after they decided to sell, but as a consequence of

---

1 Wilbert Shenk, interview by David Neufeld, 25 July 2011.

the expansion of Les Amis de l'Atelier's workshop in Châtenay-Malabry, the association had freed the Kennels to put it on the market. In the meantime, the couple had nearly sold to a number of other buyers, including a group of evangelical gypsies and an order of Orthodox nuns.[2] Nevertheless, when MMF expressed interest in the property again in 1966, the Kennels reiterated their desire to come to an arrangement with the association. Of equal significance to the future of the project was the couple's acceptance of a call to become engaged in the proposed center's activities, André as its first director.[3]

The removal of this significant personnel hurdle encouraged the MMF decision to move forward with development of a vision for the center at Hautefeuille. As a ministry of an evangelistic missionary effort, its first objective was to serve as a living testimony to the gospel. The project's witness would be built around a rural Centre d'aide par le travail, a boarding institution that would function during the workweek. Forty-eight young men with disabilities over the age of eighteen would be challenged with agricultural tasks, gardening, raising animals, and labor in a workshop, while receiving care from a permanent staff of twelve, composed primarily of French Mennonites who would be called to serve in the center. On the weekends, the property would function as an evangelical retreat center.[4] The project's planners believed that such a center would promote a model of uniting evangelism and service, which the mission wished to propagate by giving evangelical groups—many of which were hesitant about Christian social work—"the opportunity for first-hand observation of our service in the name of Christ."[5]

The mission's supporting partners were excited about the plan. Wilbert Shenk, who succeeded John H. Yoder as Assistant Secretary for Overseas Missions in 1966, confirmed that MBMC was "keenly interested"

2 Robert Witmer, "Un Rêve Réaliste," *Christ Seul*, May 1981, xviii–xix.

3 Minutes of the Executive Council of MMF, 11 February 1967, photocopy of *Cahier Officiel* of MMF, personal files of Robert Witmer, Cambridge, ON.

4 "Hautefeuille," *Christ Seul*, December 1966; and Robert Witmer, "Domaine Emmanuel de la MMF," undated. Box 2. Mennonite Board of Missions Overseas Ministry Division Data Files Part 3, 1966–1969. IV/18/013-03. Mennonite Church USA Archives. Goshen, IN.

5 Robert Witmer, "Domaine Emmanuel de la MMF," undated. Box 2. Mennonite Board of Missions Overseas Ministry Division Data Files Part 3, 1966–1969. IV/18/013-03. Mennonite Church USA Archives. Goshen, IN.

Once a hunting lodge for Paris elite on a 500-acre farm surrounded by forests, the Hautefeuille property was jointly purchased by Kennel and Rotaker families in the 1930s.

in the development of the Hautefeuille initiative.[6] The board's support was reinforced by the way the project continued to elicit the support of French Mennonites. "We believe that this involvement on their part is becoming increasingly meaningful and is the kind

of thing we very much want to have happen," Shenk wrote.[7] For its part, MMF was enthusiastic about expanding its program of service "in a distinctly evangelical environment as a witness to the love of Christ . . . in order that preaching in deed may accompany preaching in word."[8] In August 1966, after five years of work with youth with mental disabilities in Châtenay-Malabry and a long process of study and seeking God's will, MMF indicated their desire to move ahead with the purchase of the Hautefeuille property.[9]

Financing and Preparing Domaine Emmanuel

Now MMF faced the challenge of raising funds to cover the property's $120,000 purchase price and the $30,000 cost of renovation.[10] As a result of its inquiries about the development of the Foyer Fraternel workshop in

6 Wilbert Shenk to Robert Witmer, 24 October 1966. Box 2, Folder 86. Mennonite Board of Missions Overseas Ministry Division Data Files Part 3, 1966–1969. IV/18/013-03. Mennonite Church USA Archives. Goshen, IN.

7 Ibid.

8 Minutes of the MMF General Assembly, 11 March 1967, photocopy of *Cahier Officiel* of MMF, personal files of Robert Witmer, Cambridge, ON.

9 "Le Château de Hautefeuille," *Christ Seul*, October 1966, 1.

10 Wilbert Shenk, Administrative Visit Report, 20–21 July 1966. Box 2, Folder 86. Mennonite Board of Missions Overseas Ministry Division Data Files Part 3, 1966–1969. IV/18/013-03. Mennonite Church USA Archives. Goshen, IN.

In 1966 Mission Mennonite Française accepts André Kennel's offer to assume direction of its new center—Domaine Emmanuel.

Châtenay-Malabry, the association knew that the French government was willing to pay up to 80 percent of this start-up sum through later contributions to the operating budget.[11] However, given that the application deadline for the existing cinquième plan had passed in December 1965, this money would likely not become available until 1975, at the end of the subsequent cinquième plan. While this situation appeared to leave

the association with an initial capital expense it could not pay, funds were collected from a number of sources which allowed the project to proceed. Most importantly, the Kennels generously offered to accept monthly rent payments as remuneration for their property until it could be purchased using state funds.[12] In addition, after repeatedly promoting Service Épargne Mennonite in the MMF general assembly and *Christ Seul*, the association received a significant number of deposits ranging from $60 to $12,000 dollars from thirty-eight French Mennonite contributors by the end of 1968; the funds were dedicated to start-up expenses.[13] During its quest to supplement these funds, MBMC had come into contact with the North American branch of the Sudan United Mission and had offered to give control over the operation of the proposed weekend retreat center to the agency in exchange for a capital investment. These discussions, which represented the final serious attempt to establish a retreat center on the site, eventually fell through because of theological

11 Robert Witmer and Pierre Widmer, "Mission Mennonite Française," *Christ Seul*, May 1967, 15–16.

12 Robert Witmer, interview by David Neufeld, 7 June 2012.

13 Robert and Lois Witmer, Christmas Letter, 15 November 1968. Box 8, Folder 4. Mennonite Board of Missions Overseas Ministry Division Data Files Part 3, 1966–1969. IV/18/013-03. Mennonite Church USA Archives. Goshen, IN.

differences. Nevertheless, a $20,000 loan from MBMC covered the balance of the start-up costs, which were later reimbursed after the center had been approved for government subsidies.[14]

MMF had decided to proceed under this funding framework when, during Holy Week of 1967, Witmer learned through Robert Guth and Gérard Peterschmitt that there might still be an opportunity to apply for state subsidies for property purchases from the Social Welfare Department under the existing cinquième plan. The next day, he met André Kennel at the department's offices in Paris. Arriving without an appointment, they convinced the regional director, M. Gabarre, to spare a few minutes of his time. On entering the office, Kennel and Witmer found Gabarre seated at a desk, hidden behind tall stacks of folders. He was signing the final set of applications which, he explained, had taken fifteen months to compile and process and which were to be sent out the following morning to the department's minister for final approval. While clearly

exhausted, Gabarre listened carefully to his visitors. He was impressed by Kennel and Witmer's description of the MMF vision for the Hautefeuille project and reassured by their careful financial estimates. After this extended conversation, Gabarre provided an answer to the MMF representatives' prayers by confirming that there was indeed room for one final application. Seventeen months after the department's official deadline

Pictured here in the early 1970s after leaving the château in 1964, Lilianne and André Kennel and their five children in front of their refurbished farm laborers' residence

14 Wilbert Shenk, Administrative Visit Report, 20–21 July 1966; and Robert Witmer to Wilbert Shenk, 4 November 1966. Box 2, Folder 86. Mennonite Board of Missions Overseas Ministry Division Data Files Part 3, 1966–1969. IV/18/013-03. Mennonite Church USA Archives. Goshen, IN.

and hours before the applications were submitted, Kennel and Witmer successfully enrolled the Hautefeuille project in the existing cinquième plan, allowing MMF to receive reimbursement for its purchase of the Kennel estate. Overwhelmed with emotion on leaving the office, they sensed God's affirmation of the name recently chosen for the new center, which they whispered to each other: "Emmanuel," God with us.[15]

Before it opened, Domaine Emmanuel needed to be equipped and furnished. The center's organizers acquired the necessary materials from an unlikely source. In 1967, the expiration of an agreement between France and the North Atlantic Treaty Organization required the closure of NATO bases in the country. Witmer explored the possibility of obtaining materials from centers that provided North American expatriate government officials and their families with duty-free goods. But he was informed that, under the terms of international agreements, these goods could not remain in France for donation to charitable associations. They would have to be purchased, subject to a prohibitively high import tax. After tirelessly contacting various governmental agencies for nearly three months, Witmer learned that they had accepted his bid of only 2 percent of the original value of the equipment.[16] Soon thereafter, hired personnel delivered five truckloads of equipment and furnishings for the Domaine Emmanuel kitchen, cafeteria, offices, and workshops to Hautefeuille before NATO left France permanently in October.[17]

Beginning in the summer of 1967, Pax volunteers helped with the center's preparation. They installed heating and plumbing systems and kitchen equipment in the center's château, and redesigned and equipped the smaller "old château," a two-story sheepfold, and the garage, tool shop, and greenhouse. They were joined in their labor by the members of two three-week voluntary service teams composed of twenty European Mennonite youth and, after the completion of the

15 Robert Witmer, "Un Rêve Réaliste," *Christ Seul*, May 1981, xvii–xix; Robert Witmer, interview by David Neufeld, 11 July 2011; and Robert Witmer, e-mail messages to author, 5 October 2012, 16 April 2014.

16 Ibid.

17 Minutes of the MMF General Assembly, 11 March 1967, photocopy of *Cahier Officiel* of MMF, personal files of Robert Witmer, Cambridge, ON.

workshop building in Châtenay-Malabry, by a second group of Pax volunteers.[18]

In late fall 1967, the French-speaking Mennonite conference held its first-ever meeting in the Paris area. Three hundred representatives arrived to celebrate the

The main residence before the château was built in 1914

opening of Domaine Emmanuel and the completion of the new workshop facility for Les Amis de l'Atelier

in Châtenay-Malabry. On Saturday, November 11, at Hautefeuille, MMF president Pierre Widmer defended the association's mission, represented by the center, to the assembled congregation, insisting that "Jesus was made a man; Jesus was a servant; Jesus attended to the needs of men. In the same manner, we, His disciples, must love and serve in a practical way."[19] He dedicated Domaine Emmanuel to God's service and announced the commencement of its ministry.[20]

The Early Life of Domaine Emmanuel

Although Domaine Emmanuel's opening was delayed until local authorities processed final approval for the project, continued support from administrators in high places allowed the center to welcome the first fifteen (of an eventual forty-eight) men selected by the Department of Social Welfare on March 1, 1968. On learning that their children had been admitted, the parents

18 Robert and Lois Witmer, Report to sponsoring churches, 29 November 1967. Box 8, Folder 4. Mennonite Board of Missions Overseas Ministry Division Data Files Part 3, 1966–1969. IV/18/013-03. Mennonite Church USA Archives. Goshen, IN; and Robert Witmer, e-mail message to author, 23 April 2013.

19 Report of the fall 1967 Conference of the "Groupe des Églises Évangéliques–Mennonites de Langue Française," personal files of Robert Witmer, Cambridge, ON.

20 Pierre Widmer, "L'Ouverture et la Dédicace du Domaine Emmanuel," *Christ Seul*, January 1968, 15–18.

A few of the forty-eight residents of Domaine Emmanuel at work in the refurbished "sheepfold" (workshop) which began in 1968

of the young workers cried for joy.[21] Once they were residents in the center, these youth spent their days in ways much as the workers of the Centre d'aide par le travail in Châtenay-Malabry did. Most arrived at the sheltered workshops from specialized institutions for adolescents with developmental disabilities or mental health conditions. For forty hours a week, they engaged in a variety of productive activities adapted to their individual abilities. Meals, recreational activities,

and individual meetings with medical staff interrupted the workday.[22] For both centers' educators, the worker rather than their product was of primary importance. Although the youth received a salary and social security benefits, their productivity was immaterial to the central purpose of the Centre d'aide par le travail, the creation of autonomy for their participants. Denys Laruelle, an employee at Domaine Emmanuel, later explained in *Christ Seul* that "work cannot be considered solely as a means of production, but also as representing something of real value for each person: victory over physical or psychological difficulties, and, in a relationship of trust and love, the discovery in oneself of a creature made in the image of God."[23]

As facilitators of this process, the centers' staff saw their work as "the announcing of the Gospel."[24] This understanding resonated with that of the projects' founding partners, who viewed the ministry to youth

21 Pierre Widmer and Robert Witmer, "Avec la Mission Mennonite Française," *Christ Seul*, April 1968, 11.

22 Ernest Nussbaumer, "Qui Sommes-Nous?" *Christ Seul*, April 1981, ix–xi.

23 Denys Laruelle, "Une Journée Ordinaire," *Christ Seul*, May 1981, xix–xx.

24 Phillipe Manga, "Le Champ, c'est le Monde," *Christ Seul*, May 1981, xxiii, xxiv.

with disabilities as a testimony not only to the parents and families of the workers but also to state authorities and broader society. The implementation of this vision was not without difficulties. Despite organizers' best efforts to integrate new workers into a team, interpersonal relationships among the personnel were often characterized by conflict during Domaine Emmanuel's first year of operation. Director André Kennel's annual report described a period of unexpected difficulties, for the forty-eight workers forced to adapt to new roles and for an uninitiated and sometimes inexperienced staff which had been unable to cohere into a community of mutual trust.[25] To some degree, conflict at Hautefeuille was an inevitable product of an intense communal life in an isolated and unfamiliar setting. However, André Kennel's wish to resign as director of the center in the face of the tensions revealed the seriousness of the circumstances.[26] Pierre Widmer's pastoral interven-

tion helped ease tensions, but it became evident to the project's partners that the wholesome and mutually supportive staff environment they had hoped would bolster the center's testimony was not taking shape as envisioned.

The situation at Hautefeuille drew further attention to an ongoing concern of MMF and its institutions: a lack of personnel fit and willing to carry out the association's vision. The two-pronged nature of the partners' missionary program, to witness to the gospel by responding to the world's spiritual and physical needs, complicated the search for capable staff. To address this problem over the next decade, the association pursued various initiatives to promote service in its ministries among French Mennonites. The frequency of calls for personnel in *Christ Seul*, first made by Anne Sommermeyer in 1958, increased. Individuals with "a deep Christian conviction and a sincere desire to communicate the love of Christ" were often invited to consider missionary service in MMF institutions.[27] The association preferred individuals with specialized training in the care of youth with developmental disabilities

25 André Kennel, Domaine Emmanuel Annual Report, November 1968–September 1969. Box 2, Folder 83. Mennonite Board of Missions Overseas Ministry Division Data Files Part 3, 1966–1969. IV/18/013-03. Mennonite Church USA Archives. Goshen, IN.

26 Pierre Widmer to André Kennel and Domaine Emmanuel personnel, 28 October 1968, personal files of Robert Witmer,

Cambridge, ON.

27 "Au nom de Christ," *Christ Seul*, December 1972, 14–15.

or mental health conditions, but did not require these qualifications for all positions. The door was left open to a wide variety of candidates.[28] The directors of MMF social projects made appeals in person, visiting Mennonite congregations to provide information and encourage young people to consider dedicating their academic preparation and careers to service and mission.[29] Events such as the inaugurations of new buildings in Paris also helped to raise the profile of opportunities for missionary service there.[30] MMF's overwhelmingly positive experience with the service of Pax volunteers led Witmer, on the association's behalf, to explore the possibility of increased participation by North American personnel in MMF projects. MBMC considered creating an Overseas Mission Associate position for a

volunteer with specialized training in social work, but this idea was discarded.[31]

In September 1973, the MMF general assembly invited Commandant Jolivot from the Salvation Army to speak about the personnel challenges inherent in creation and operation of Christian social ministries. Jolivot singled out MMF institutions as unique among similar evangelical projects in France in that 80 percent of staff were Christian.[32] He encouraged MMF, working from this position of relative strength, to enhance the spiritual lives of existing staff by organizing team-building exercises and to facilitate formation of potential servants by providing vocational training. The general assembly responded to this challenge by adopting a resolution to create a specialized school to

28 Robert Witmer, "Mission de Châtenay-Malabry," *Christ Seul*, February 1965, 7–8.

29 Marlin Miller, "Report to MBM Overseas Committee," 30 March 1972. Box 2, Folder 2. Mennonite Board of Missions Overseas Ministry Division Data Files Part 4, 1970–1974. IV/18/013-04. Mennonite Church USA Archives. Goshen, IN.

30 Théo Hege, e-mail message to author, 15 June 2012.

31 Robert Witmer to Peter Dyck, 24 January 1969; Robert Witmer to Wilbert Shenk, 13 February 1969; and Wilbert Shenk to Robert Witmer, 18 February 1969. Box 2, Folder 83. Mennonite Board of Missions Overseas Ministry Division Data Files Part 3, 1966–1969. IV/18/013-03. Mennonite Church USA Archives. Goshen, IN.

32 Commandant Jolivot, "Recrutement et Formation de Collaborateurs dans nos Oeuvres Évangéliques," *Christ Seul*, January/February 1974, 9–13.

train personnel for evangelical social projects.[33] Soon thereafter, MMF joined other evangelical groups in the formation of Action Sociale et Évangile (ASEv), an educational institution that sought to accomplish this goal. Through ASEv, the staffing of MMF centers engendered institutional cooperation with other evangelical groups.[34]

These initiatives to recruit Mennonite young people met with mixed success. Nevertheless, ongoing staffing difficulties at Domaine Emmanuel did not alter the directors' purpose for the center. They considered Hautefeuille a unique mission field, one without defined limits.[35] Staff shared their testimony by caring for youth with developmental disabilities or mental health conditions, but also hoped to have an impact on the broader community in which they lived. In 1972, the directors'

and staff's concern for evangelism and their desire to enrich the center's spiritual life led to the creation of a small community of faith. Functioning independently of Domaine Emmanuel, Église Évangélique de Hautefeuille incorporated the center's staff, residents, and families from the surrounding area.[36] The struggles involved in starting any new congregation were, in this case, complicated by the participation of youth with developmental disabilities or mental health conditions. What did evangelism, conversion, baptism, and church membership mean for these members?[37] Both at work and at church, the Domaine Emmanuel staff, like that of the workshop in Châtenay-Malabry, continuously confronted questions of how best to communicate the gospel's good news to the center's residents.

MCC Pax Involvement at Domaine Emmanuel

The church's founding coincided with construction of more housing for Domaine Emmanuel staff. Art

33 Minutes of the MMF General Assembly, 30 September 1973, photocopy of *Cahier Officiel* of MMF, personal files of Robert Witmer, Cambridge, ON.

34 Marlin Miller, "Report to MBM Overseas Committee," 30 March 1972. Box 2, Folder 2. Mennonite Board of Missions Overseas Ministry Division Data Files Part 4, 1970–1974. IV/18/013-04. Mennonite Church USA Archives. Goshen, IN.

35 André Kennel, "Domaine Emmanuel," *Christ Seul*, January 1978, 28.

36 Gilbert Klopfenstein, "Comment vit une église solidaire d'une oeuvre?" *Christ Seul*, February 1988, 19–20.

37 Marlin Miller, "Report to MBM Overseas Committee," 30 March 1972. Box 2, Folder 2. Mennonite Board of Missions Overseas Ministry Division Data Files Part 4, 1970–1974. IV/18/013-04. Mennonite Church USA Archives. Goshen, IN.

Art Neuenschwander, André Kennel, and Secretary J. P. Davillerd checking the blueprints for Pax construction of the Canadian houses

Neuenschwander, a college student from the United States, arrived in Paris in September 1970 to join a Pax team charged with building new living space. In many ways, Neuenschwander's experience exemplified that of many Pax volunteers who worked for the missionary effort in Paris. At the time, the military draft in the US obligated conscientious objectors not enrolled in university studies to enlist in some form of alternative service. Given these conditions, Neuenschwander

sought out an experience abroad where he could put his skills to good use. His motivations paralleled those of Pax volunteer John Ray Kennel, who explained on his application form that "I wish to serve in Pax in order to

In front of the Canadian house which became the office of Domaine Emmanuel in 1972. Left to right: Herb Goulet, representing Dumez-Campeau (Canada housing promotion in France), Lilianne Kennel, André Kennel, Robert Witmer, and Art Neuenschwander

serve people rather than destroy them. I feel the need for a worthwhile alternate service experience which is not merely one of convenience for myself. I also think there is a need for international understanding as promoted by Pax."[38]

After arriving in France, Neuenschwander lived at Foyer Fraternel and enrolled in intensive language studies at Alliance Française. Basic knowledge of French allowed him to build relationships within the community in Châtenay-Malabry and engage in the local congregation's life. In Hautefeuille, he lived in the château in cramped conditions. Although the primary task of the Pax team at Domaine Emmanuel was construction, volunteers engaged in a variety of activities, helping out with excursions for the center's boarders, for instance. In the Pax volunteers' orientation, supervisor Peter Dyck had been adamant about the need to adapt to whatever work was offered. The spirit in which the volunteers carried out the work was more important than the work itself, he believed.[39]

Three Pax colleagues on the wall: James Burkhart, Steve Diller, and Larry Thim

Neuenschwander's experience differed from that of other Pax volunteers in France in the level of responsibility he was given. The twenty-year-old volunteer was asked to help coordinate expansion of the Domaine Emmanuel housing capacity. Soon after Neuenschwander's arrival at Hautefeuille, Robert Witmer learned of a house-building project in the nearby town of Igny, sponsored jointly by the French and Canadian governments, that was willing to sell its excess building supplies to the center. Using funds that had been collected for development of the Hautefeuille property,

---

38 "Mennonite Central Committee summary of Personnel Information Form: John Ray Kennel," 31 March 1969, personal files of Robert Witmer, Cambridge, ON.

39 Art Neuenschwander, interview by David Neufeld, 20 July 2011.

By eliminating plans for garages for the three Canadian houses, the Pax volunteers were able to economize enough on building material and floor space to make four complete units.

Domaine Emmanuel purchased these materials at cost from the builders, who also provided detailed copies of their building plans free of charge. From an office given to him by André Kennel, Neuenschwander directed the local Pax team in erecting five Canadian-style wood homes. In order to supervise the project's completion, Neuenschwander returned after his wedding in 1973 for one year as paid MMF staff.[40]

---

40 Ibid. Merl E. Lehman, "Ohio Youth Returns with Bride, Paxmen Serve at "Domaine Emmanuel," *Mennonite Weekly*

Developments in Châtenay-Malabry, 1966–73

In Châtenay-Malabry, Les Amis de l'Atelier achieved a period of stability under director Théo Hege's leadership. As a member of the MMF executive council, Hege made frequent trips to eastern France to promote and mobilize financial support for the association's projects among Mennonite individuals and congregations, many of whom still saw an organized response to society's basic needs as the charge of the state.[41] In 1966, Les Amis de l'Atelier had modified its rules to allow all sympathetic individuals, primarily parents of workers, to join the association. In one year, its membership jumped from twenty-one to fifty-two.[42]

Despite the broadening of its base of financial and moral support, Les Amis de l'Atelier remained inextricably linked to Foyer Fraternel. Church members formed the core of the association's membership and

---

Review, 11 January 1973; and Robert Witmer, e-mail message to author, 5 October 2012.

41 Théo Hege, e-mail message to author, 15 June 2012.

42 Théo Hege, "Rapport Moral" of "Les Amis de l'Atelier," 1965. Box 2, Folder 86. Mennonite Board of Missions Overseas Ministry Division Data Files Part 3, 1966–1969. IV/18/013-03. Mennonite Church USA Archives. Goshen, IN.

leadership. Many of the workshop's staff participated in the life of the congregation, and the workshop continued to use the church's kitchen, dining area, and courtyard during meal and recreation periods.[43] The concerns of the workshop were those of the church, and vice versa.[44] While this arrangement ensured the congregation's spiritual direction of the project, shared space and administration continued to cause occasional tensions.[45]

The workshop consumed much of Foyer Fraternel's energies, but it remained only one aspect of the church's work. By the early 1970s, the congregation benefited from the presence of a core of committed members who offered continuity to its shared life.[46] The membership's diversity continued to challenge the faith community's leaders, who worked continuously to turn the congregation's unique composition into a source of enrichment, balance, and strength.[47] A persistent focus on outreach manifested itself in the continuation of evangelistic initiatives. For instance, the first Sunday worship of every month focused specifically on evangelism.[48] Additionally, as it had since 1962, the congregation invited the workshop's workers and their families to attend the annual Christmas program.[49] French classes for thirty North Africans continued on a weekly basis.[50] Finally, the church created a coffee bar, staffed by four Christian students, as a drop-in center for community youth. It regularly drew a crowd of between thirty and sixty young people for singing and informal conversation. In 1973, as a sign of the congregation's growing maturity, Foyer Fraternel called Roger Kennel and Mennonite Board of Missions worker Marlin

---

43 Robert Witmer, e-mail message to author, 5 October 2012.

44 Théo Hege, e-mail message to author, 15 June 2012.

45 Marlin Miller, "Report to MBM Overseas Committee," 30 March 1972. Box 2, Folder 2. Mennonite Board of Missions Overseas Ministry Division Data Files Part 4, 1970–1974. IV/18/013-04. Mennonite Church USA Archives. Goshen, IN.

46 Ibid.

47 Robert Witmer, "Report, Mission Mennonite Française," 1968, personal files of Robert Witmer, Cambridge, ON.

48 Marlin Miller, "Report to MBM Overseas Committee," 30 March 1972. Box 2, Folder 2. Mennonite Board of Missions Overseas Ministry Division Data Files Part 4, 1970–1974. IV/18/013-04. Mennonite Church USA Archives. Goshen, IN.

49 Robert Witmer, "Report, Mission Mennonite Française," 1968, personal files of Robert Witmer, Cambridge, ON.

50 Mme Paris and Théo Hege, "Châtenay-Malabry," *Christ Seul*, January 1967, 22–24.

Miller to serve as the church's first elders.[51] They, like elders in other French Mennonite congregations, were invested by the community with authority to preside over communion, baptisms, marriages, and other significant church ceremonies.

Partners Explore New Missionary Opportunities, 1975

For a number of reasons, the mid-1970s represented a "strategic juncture" for MMF.[52] First, the association encountered a lull in program development. Foyer Fraternel was experiencing healthy maturation and growth, and the two Centres d'aides par le travail created under MMF auspices were functioning well and had nearly paid off their debts.

Second, in the fall of 1974, French members of Foyer Fraternel took over responsibility for the congregation's pastoral ministry. MBM policy precluded North American missionaries from becoming permanent pastors of the congregations in which they participated. In keeping with these expectations, the Witmers had first proffered their resignation as pastors of the church in January 1971. The congregation had not accepted this proposal.[53] On the Witmers' return, MBM staff continued to promote the idea of a transition to local leadership. The board recognized that as long as the congregation relied on North American missionaries for personnel needs, its progress would be stunted.[54] Thus, starting in 1972, the Witmers ministered as members of a pastoral team. Two years later, their fifteen-year term as pastors of Foyer Fraternel concluded. This step did not mean an overnight transition from missionary support to independence. The Witmers would stay on as active contributors to the life and theological ori-

51 Robert Witmer, "Mission Mennonite Française, Rapport Moral," *Christ Seul*, November 1973, 10.

52 Wilbert Shenk, "Administrative Visit Report, France, February 21–23," 20 March 1975. Box 2, Folder 11. Mennonite Board of Missions Overseas Ministry Division Data Files Part 5, 1975–1979. IV/18/013-05. Mennonite Church USA Archives. Goshen, IN.

53 Wilbert Shenk to Robert Witmer, 6 January 1971; and Robert Witmer to Wilbert Shenk, 12 January 1971. Box 4, Folder 47. Mennonite Board of Missions Overseas Ministry Division Data Files Part 4, 1970–1974. IV/18/013-04. Mennonite Church USA Archives. Goshen, IN.

54 Marlin Miller, "Report to MBM Overseas Committee," 30 March 1972. Box 2, Folder 2. Mennonite Board of Missions Overseas Ministry Division Data Files Part 4, 1970–1974. IV/18/013-04. Mennonite Church USA Archives. Goshen, IN.

entation of the congregation for more than a decade.[55] Nevertheless, as a result of these developments, MMF needed to orient their executive secretary's future work.

Third, the leadership transition at Foyer Fraternel was followed by significant changes in the MMF administrative makeup. In 1975, Pierre Widmer resigned as the association's president because of health concerns. Widmer's passion for mission and his openness to intercultural collaboration had been instrumental in the formation of the partnership between MMF and MBMC. His spiritual leadership, mediation skills, and pastoral support had been a vital element in the success of the association's work. Thus, his absence left a significant leadership and visioning void that needed to be filled. The impact of Widmer's departure was compounded by the resignation of Robert Witmer as the association's executive secretary, tendered to new president Bernard Klopfenstein at the association's general assembly in 1975. MMF was a French association, and it was an appropriate time for a French Mennonite to become the association's principal worker, Witmer contended.[56] Since 1958, Witmer had occupied a central position in the partnership. As MBM missionary and sole full-time employee of MMF, he had assumed major responsibility for the association's program development, carrying out its vision while serving as the primary channel of communication between his sponsoring entities. His resignation, although not accepted by the association until 1983, suggested that this phase was coming to a conclusion.

Wilbert Shenk's administrative visit to France in February 1975 offered representatives of MMF and MBM an opportunity to reconnect, take stock of progress made, and shape a joint vision for the future. The North American board, while contributing to this latter process, wished to support rather than determine its outcome.[57] Over more than two decades of collab-

---

55 Wilbert Shenk, "Administrative Visit Report, France, February 21–23," 20 March 1975. Box 2, Folder 11. Mennonite Board of Missions Overseas Ministry Division Data Files Part 5, 1975–1979. IV/18/013-05. Mennonite Church USA Archives. Goshen, IN.

56 Minutes of the MMF General Assembly, 1 November 1975, photocopy of *Cahier Officiel* of MMF, personal files of Robert Witmer, Cambridge, ON.

57 Wilbert Shenk, "Administrative Visit Report, France, February 21–23," 20 March 1975. Box 2, Folder 11. Mennonite Board of Missions Overseas Ministry Division Data Files Part 5, 1975–1979. IV/18/013-05. Mennonite Church USA Archives. Goshen, IN.

oration, the basic components of the partnership had not changed. Through Shenk, MBM reasserted its commitment to work in France exclusively through MMF, which maintained administrative control and supervision over joint projects in the country.[58] At the same time, elements of the partners' relationship had evolved. Although MBM continued to provide a $4,500 annual subsidy to MMF for staff travel and office expenses, as it had done since 1960, MMF had taken over responsibility for the majority of program costs.[59] Furthermore, the prospect of Witmer's resignation from the MMF executive council, fully in keeping with MBM's expectations, implied an alteration in the partners' methods of collaborating and interacting.

In their evaluation of the partnership's fruits, both parties agreed that the ministry to youth with developmental and mental health conditions was a pioneering success that had changed lives and served as a witness to the broader evangelical community and society.[60] Increasingly, the association's involvement in social work had encouraged interaction with directors of other Mennonite social institutions. Ongoing discussions permitted administrators to share experiences and pursue greater coordination of their efforts.[61] The integration of the work of Parisian Mennonites into the consciousness of Mennonites in eastern France was undoubtedly a positive development. Yet, Shenk noted, the MMF membership believed that the association's focus on the development of the workshops had resulted in neglect of evangelism, MMF's first objective. "Can we direct a part of our efforts in the direction of evangelism in the traditional sense of the word?" MMF general assembly participants had wondered.[62]

---

58 Ibid.

59 Minutes of the MMF General Assembly, 20 February 1963, photocopy of *Cahier Officiel* of MMF, personal files of Robert Witmer, Cambridge, ON.

60 Marlin Miller, "Report to MBM Overseas Committee," 30 March 1972. Box 2, Folder 2. Mennonite Board of Missions Overseas Ministry Division Data Files Part 4, 1970–1974. IV/18/013-04. Mennonite Church USA Archives. Goshen, IN.

61 Minutes of the General Assemblies of the MMF, 11 November 1970 and 11 November 1971, photocopy of *Cahier Officiel* of MMF, personal files of Robert Witmer, Cambridge, ON.

62 Minutes of the MMF General Assembly, 11 November 1970, photocopy of *Cahier Officiel* of MMF, personal files of

In a speech to the first joint conference of French- and German-speaking Mennonites in France in March 1975, outgoing MMF president Pierre Widmer expressed the association's desire to rededicate itself to church planting and evangelism. He challenged the audience to support a new "home missions" thrust, staffed by workers expelled from newly independent Chad and by young French Mennonite students who for years had been frustrated in their attempts to find pastoral or missionary assignments in France after completing biblical and theological studies.[63]

Shenk wholeheartedly supported this vision and believed that MBM personnel in France would work to pursue it. Both partners agreed that Foyer Fraternel provided an excellent model for how domestic mission efforts might proceed, and might serve as a base from which new projects could be launched. Over the next decade, the partners' renewed emphasis on evangelism and church planting manifested itself in three ways: the foreign student ministry of Foyer Grebel, financial

support of European evangelistic projects, and development of work with individuals with special spiritual and social needs in the Parisian suburb of Verrières-le-Buisson.

A Ministry to Foreign Students in Paris: Foyer Grebel, 1965–82

Plans for a Peace Center in Paris

Foyer Grebel was created by MMF in 1977 with the primary goal of "proclaiming, in word and deed, God's salvation and love given to us in Jesus" by serving the physical and spiritual needs of foreign students in Paris.[64] The ministry grew primarily out of a Mennonite Central Committee effort in the mid-1960s to establish a peace center in Paris. MCC's Peace Section, an agency dedicated to peace promotion, study, and education, had perceived a need for a Mennonite peace witness in Paris. Existing pacifist organizations in the city were either "Catholic" or "communist," and had little

Robert Witmer, Cambridge, ON.
63 Wilbert Shenk, "Administrative Visit Report, France, February 21–23," 20 March 1975. Box 2, Folder 11. Mennonite Board of Missions Overseas Ministry Division Data Files

Part 5, 1975–1979. IV/18/013-05. Mennonite Church USA Archives. Goshen, IN.
64 Neal Blough, "Le Foyer Grebel," Christ Seul, January 1977, 4–7.

Marlin and Ruthann Miller lived in Paris from 1968 to 1974 and laid the groundwork for the establishment of a program for African Christian university students, which served as a precursor to Foyer Grebel in Saint Maurice. The initiative involved a partnership of MMF, MCC, and MBM.

interest in promoting conscientious objection.[65] Beginning in March 1965, the agency had considered establishing a center that would give leadership to France's 250 conscientious objectors, carry out a teaching program, and sponsor seminars and conversations with other churches and peace groups. This meeting place would extend its comprehensive Christian peace witness to the local community by offering lodging to foreign students. Between 90,000 and 100,000 such students lived in Paris, many of them from former French colonies in Africa, and most suffered the consequences of the city's severe housing shortage. The center's proponents hoped that any future student residence could be connected to a Mennonite community.[66]

Peace Section representative Marlin Miller contacted Robert Witmer about the plan in the summer of 1965. Over the years, African students had arrived continuously at Foyer Fraternel looking for a place to

65 Memorandum, Marlin Miller to MCC Peace Section, MBMC, MMF, Peace Section European Committee, DMFK, Vredesgroep, 21 January 1966. Box 2, Folder 86. Mennonite Board of Missions Overseas Ministry Division Data Files Part 3, 1966–1969. IV/18/013-03. Mennonite Church USA Archives. Goshen, IN.

66 Ibid.

live.[67] Thus, Witmer confirmed, "the type of center you project and your reasons for considering location in the Paris area correspond realistically with the situation as we see it from here."[68] Miller's request arrived during MMF consideration of possible uses for the neighboring Rebiffé property; consequently, Witmer envisioned the possibility of combining a peace and student center with a permanent workshop building in Châtenay-Malabry. The benefits seemed clear. The two projects would be able to share space and costs, and the peace center would be linked to an existing Mennonite church that was attempting to model the unification of Christian testimony and service that MCC Peace Section wished to promote.[69] MBMC supported Witmer's proposal, seeing the peace and student center as "part and parcel" of what the board was trying to accomplish in Paris.[70]

In January 1966, Miller visited Paris to explore this proposal further. With Witmer, he consulted with Protestant student ministries, conscientious objectors, public officials, and an architect. Following these meetings, the men proposed creation of a financially self-sustaining center to house thirty students in Châtenay-Malabry. The project would be led by an MCC Peace Section worker who, before taking on a full-time role at the complex, would hold a half-time teaching and ministry position at Foyer Fraternel. "At Châtenay-Malabry with a workshop for retarded children, an already existing congregation, a student community and a peace center, the various aspects of a living Christian witness would be given visible expression," an internal MCC Peace Section memo read. "There would be a preaching and teaching ministry, a service to youth for whom no one cares, a witness to students and development of group life among them and a specifically

67 Neal Blough, interview by David Neufeld, 16 July 2011.

68 Robert Witmer to Marlin Miller, 16 August 1965. Box 4, Folder 25. Mennonite Board of Missions Overseas Ministry Division Data Files Part 2, 1956–1965. IV/18/013-02. Mennonite Church USA Archives. Goshen, IN.

69 Robert Witmer to Marlin Miller, 16 August 1965. Box 4, Folder 25. Mennonite Board of Missions Overseas Ministry Division Data Files Part 2, 1956–1965. IV/18/013-02. Mennonite Church USA Archives. Goshen, IN.

70 Wilbert Shenk, interview by David Neufeld, 25 July 2011.

Christian peace witness within this context and reaching beyond into the community."[71]

One month later, Miller presented this integrated proposal to the MMF general assembly. He received a lukewarm reaction, with various members questioning the missionary value of the project.[72] Furthermore, it soon became clear that a number of factors, including the Paris mission's focus on the newly created center at Hautefeuille, would postpone construction of any large integrated facility at Châtenay-Malabry.[73] Without the potential for shared space and costs, the working assumption that the center could be financially self-

Front door signage at Foyer Grebel

supporting was no longer realistic. Despite these setbacks, both MCC Peace Section and MBMC believed it made sense to move ahead with a ministry to foreign students in Paris, even without a building. In July, they extended a joint call to Miller to study the needs of foreign students in the city and to explore how a center might best respond to them. His term was to last six to seven years, his costs covered equally by the two sponsoring parties.[74] In addition to pursuing establish-

71 Memorandum, Marlin Miller to MCC Peace Section, MBMC, MMF, Peace Section European Committee, DMFK, Vredesgroep, 21 January 1966. Box 2, Folder 86. Mennonite Board of Missions Overseas Ministry Division Data Files Part 3, 1966–1969. IV/18/013-03. Mennonite Church USA Archives. Goshen, IN.

72 Minutes of the MMF General Assembly, 5 February 1966, photocopy of *Cahier Officiel* of MMF, personal files of Robert Witmer, Cambridge, ON.

73 Marlin Miller to Edgar Metzler, 27 August 1966. Box 5, Folder 65. Mennonite Board of Missions Overseas Ministry Division Data Files Part 3, 1966–1969. IV/18/013-03. Mennonite Church USA Archives. Goshen, IN.

74 Wilbert Shenk to Marlin Miller, 20 July 1966. Box 5, Folder 65. Mennonite Board of Missions Overseas Ministry Division

ment of a center, Miller would participate in European peace discussions, witness to students, relate to French Mennonites, and teach at Foyer Fraternel.[75] Because of his experience working in a similar role, John H. Yoder offered to serve as a resource person for the work.[76] In his capacity as an MBMC worker, Miller would operate under the supervision of MMF, which despite its hesitations now lent support to his efforts.

Miller arrived in Paris with his wife, Ruthann, in May 1968. In his work, Miller adopted an informal and flexible approach. Instead of tying his efforts to a particular institutional framework or a specific location, he organized Bible study groups, seminars, and retreats around student interest and availability.[77] Miller offered students help in finding adequate housing. He also made a concerted effort to establish contacts with a variety of Christian organizations working with foreign students in Paris.

Miller developed his most fruitful friendships with African students and student organizations. In 1970, he became involved with Association Chrétienne des Étudiants Africains Protestants (ACEAP), an organization founded in the 1950s by African students studying in Paris; its aim was mutual support and edification. In 1973, the association invited Miller to become its administrative assistant. In 1972, he met Tshinabu Tshimika, a Mennonite Brethren student at the Evangelical Faculty at Vaux-sur-Seine, who, with the missionary's encouragement, began attending Foyer Fraternel and participating in its coffee bar ministry. Through Jacques Baumann, a Swiss Mennonite missionary expelled from Chad, Miller got to know Aboh Lambert Danrhé and

---

Data Files Part 3, 1966–1969. IV/18/013-03. Mennonite Church USA Archives. Goshen, IN.

75 Wilbert Shenk, "Marlin Miller Paris Assignment," 6 February 1967. Box 5, Folder 65. Mennonite Board of Missions Overseas Ministry Division Data Files Part 3, 1966–1969. IV/18/013-03. Mennonite Church USA Archives. Goshen, IN.

76 Wilbert Shenk to Robert Witmer, 20 December 1966. Box 2, Folder 86. Mennonite Board of Missions Overseas Ministry Division Data Files Part 3, 1966–1969. IV/18/013-03. Mennonite Church USA Archives. Goshen, IN.

77 Wilbert Shenk, "Administrative Visit Report," 29–30 March 1969. Box 2, Folder 83. Mennonite Board of Missions Overseas Ministry Division Data Files Part 3, 1966–1969. IV/18/013-03. Mennonite Church USA Archives. Goshen, IN.

his family.[78] Both Tshimika and Danrhé later became heavily involved in the development of Foyer Grebel, as board member and director, respectively.

The Partners Offer Support for Creation of a Student Lodging Center

When Miller left France in August 1974, he made it clear that any successful ministry oriented toward helping African students in Paris needed to provide lodging, especially for married students.[79] Apartments were nearly impossible to find, and if available, were dispersed throughout the city. Furthermore, the clear majority of landlords Miller contacted were unwilling to accept African tenants. Without a shared living space in an accepting environment, the formation of a cohesive student community was not feasible. "It seems to us that, based on past experiences, a small welcoming center with temporary lodging and meeting space

would facilitate a variety of efforts to serve," he reported.[80]

MBM replaced Marlin and Ruthann Miller with Larry and Eleanor Miller, who retained MCC Peace

Eleanor and Larry (pictured here) Miller were the first of two young couples sent to Paris by Mennonite Board of Missions in 1975 to develop the student center.

78 Marlin Miller, "La MMF et les Étudiants Africains à Paris," *Christ Seul*, April 1974, 11–12.

79 MMF Report, "Foyer Grebel, Centre d'Accueil pour Étudiants Étrangers," 15 January 1977, Foyer Grebel Archive, Centre Mennonite de Paris, France.

80 Marlin Miller, "La MMF et les Étudiants Africains à Paris," *Christ Seul*, April 1974, 11–12.

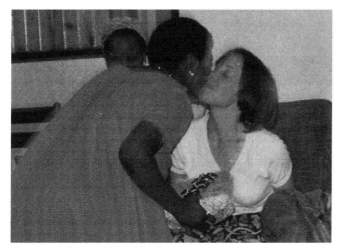

Eleanor Miller, embraced by Françoise Awezaï

Section responsibilities, and Neal and Janie Blough. Both couples arrived in Paris from the United States in 1975. The Millers were immediately tasked with finding suitable real estate for a student center. The cost of such a building, between $200,000 and $300,000, was much higher than MBM had anticipated.[81] Despite

---

81 Larry Miller to J. D. Graber, 2 May 1975. Box 4. Mennonite Board of Missions Overseas Ministry Division Data Files Part 6, 1980–1984. IV/18/013-06. Mennonite Church USA Archives. Goshen, IN.

the hesitations of other senior administrators, Wilbert Shenk supported Marlin Miller's initial recommendation. The decision to create a lodging center had grown out of a thorough exploration of the immediate needs of foreign students in Paris, he argued. The lodging and meeting center, despite its significant cost, was essential to the creation of a student community connected to a Mennonite congregation. "For us there is the further consideration that we essentially reject the

Neal and Janie Blough arrived in Paris in 1975 as Mennonite Board of Missions workers assigned to the projected student center. They have remained in France through the publication of this work (2016), contributing to a variety of church ministries.

individualistic approach and believe that people ought to be drawn into a circle of believing Christians," he continued.[82]

Still, MBM's willingness to make a substantial financial and personnel commitment to the project hinged on a clarification of what it meant to work closely with MMF on the creation of a student center.[83] Although MMF had officially sponsored Marlin Miller's exploratory work, the depth of its members' interest in the project remained unclear. Miller had been hesitant to pass over complete supervisory control of his work to MMF because of "different outlooks" on youth culture and cooperation with other evangelical groups.[84] Shenk

recognized that MMF had felt somewhat distant from the student witness. Moving forward, however, any purchase of property would be administered through the French association. More importantly, Shenk asserted, "the integrity of our relationship with MMF is jeopardized when we do not work with them in a clear-cut manner in an important area of program. There has been growth in rapport during the past 20 years and I believe there is increasingly less justification for fencing off certain areas as too controversial for the French and Americans to work together."[85] In Shenk's view, the best way to change the assumption that the student project was "a North American preserve" was to make MMF the locus for basic program decisions in the future. MBM had no interest in saddling MMF with a program in which it had no interest. Internal MMF discussions about its willingness to invest capital in a ministry to foreign students would help determine the association's level of commitment to the plan, Shenk believed.[86]

82 Wilbert Shenk to J. D. Graber and Lawrence Greaser, 6 May 1975. Box 4. Mennonite Board of Missions Overseas Ministry Division Data Files Part 6, 1980–1984. IV/18/013-06. Mennonite Church USA Archives. Goshen, IN.

83 Larry Miller to Wilbert Shenk, 30 May 1975. Box 4. Mennonite Board of Missions Overseas Ministry Division Data Files Part 6, 1980–1984. IV/18/013-06. Mennonite Church USA Archives. Goshen, IN.

84 Wilbert Shenk to J. D. Graber and Lawrence Greaser, 6 May 1975. Box 4. Mennonite Board of Missions Overseas Ministry Division Data Files Part 6, 1980–1984. IV/18/013-06. Mennonite Church USA Archives. Goshen, IN.

85 Ibid.

86 Wilbert Shenk to Larry Miller, 4 June 1975. Box 4. Mennonite Board of Missions Overseas Ministry Division Data Files Part 6, 1980–1984. IV/18/013-06. Mennonite Church USA Archives. Goshen, IN.

MMF responded favorably to MBM's proposal to re-configure the student center's decision-making framework. Writing to J. D. Graber, Bernard Klopfenstein agreed to look for ways for MMF to become directly involved in the work started by MBM. Although MMF involvement over the past years had been limited because of "a variety of difficulties," in the future the association wished "to work in close collaboration with MBM. We will always be happy to benefit from your past experience and to help you whenever possible."[87] In September 1975, the MMF executive council studied plans for the project's development and agreed to submit them to both the French Mennonite Mission Committee and the MMF general assembly. Both bodies supported establishment of a student witness in Paris, seeing it as a new form of action at a time when countries in Africa were closing their borders to European missionaries.[88] "What a wonderful opportunity to 'make disciples . . . of all nations' among the great number of students that come to our country," the general assembly meeting's report concluded.[89]

After both partners had committed themselves to moving forward with the project, clear administrative roles needed to be established. Larry Miller and MMF representatives discussed two potential arrangements. First, they explored the possibility of full French control over the project. Under this scenario, MMF would solicit MBM funding and personnel as it saw fit. The French association preferred a second option, which envisaged a jointly administered, funded, and staffed program secured by a long-term commitment from both partners. This arrangement sought to distribute the project's financial and personnel burdens equitably. Both parties agreed that such a project would provide an example for cooperative Mennonite mission efforts in other places, modeling an alternative to the choice between foreign control and the quick departure of missionaries in order to avoid paternalism. Furthermore, Miller reported, the center "could make more

---

87 Bernard Klopfenstein to J. D. Graber, 25 July 1975. Mennonite Board of Missions Overseas Ministry Division Data Files Part 5, 1975–1979. IV/18/013-05. Mennonite Church USA Archives. Goshen, IN.

88 MMF Report, "Foyer Grebel, Centre d'Accueil pour Étudiants Étrangers," 15 January 1977, Foyer Grebel Archive, Centre Mennonite de Paris, France.

89 Minutes of the MMF General Assembly, 1 November 1975, photocopy of *Cahier Officiel* of MMF, personal files of Robert Witmer, Cambridge, ON.

visible the reality of Christian unity across national and theological boundaries, a reality we are trying to communicate to those students with whom we come in contact." Larry Miller thought tensions might arise from the integration of diverse perspectives, but he supported a "long-term commitment to structurally shared responsibility for the project."[90] MBM decided readily to accept the MMF proposal. "We believe that the cooperation of the past twenty-five years has proven to be productive and mutually enriching. We have confidence that this venture can be in that same tradition," Shenk confirmed.[91]

In February 1976, a committee began to search for an appropriate building for the student center. MMF proposed that MBM furnish one-third of the purchase cost and half of the personnel and operating costs.[92] The French association, using the proceeds from the sale of the MMF property in Clamart, would contribute equal support.[93] The final third of the capital expenses was to come from French and Swiss Mennonite contributions, raised under the auspices of the French Mennonite Mission Committee.[94] All parties approved this arrangement. By May, the search committee had selected a property in the suburb of Saint Maurice, with excellent access to transportation routes that would make

90 Larry Miller to Wilbert Shenk, 20 February 1976. Box 2, Folder 11. Mennonite Board of Missions Overseas Ministry Division Data Files Part 5, 1975–1979. IV/18/013-05. Mennonite Church USA Archives. Goshen, IN.

91 Wilbert Shenk to Robert Witmer, 12 March 1976. Box 2, Folder 11. Mennonite Board of Missions Overseas Ministry Division Data Files Part 5, 1975–1979. IV/18/013-05. Mennonite Church USA Archives. Goshen, IN.

92 Larry Miller to Wilbert Shenk, 20 February 1976. Box 2, Folder 11. Mennonite Board of Missions Overseas Ministry Division Data Files Part 5, 1975–1979. IV/18/013-05. Mennonite Church USA Archives. Goshen, IN.

93 Minutes of the MMF General Assembly, 31 October 1976, photocopy of Cahier Officiel of MMF, personal files of Robert Witmer, Cambridge, ON.

94 Robert Witmer to MMF Administrative Council members, 17 September 1976. Box 2, Folder 11. Mennonite Board of Missions Overseas Ministry Division Data Files Part 5, 1975–1979. IV/18/013-05. Mennonite Church USA Archives. Goshen, IN.

the center a more attractive home to students. MMF purchased the building at 13, Val d'Osne in July.[95]

Envisioning and Preparing for a Ministry for Foreign Students

MMF called for the formation of a local council with representatives from the French association, MBM, Foyer Fraternel, and the African student population and charged it with administration of the center's

Student room at Foyer Grebel

Student meal at Foyer Grebel

95 MMF Report, "Foyer Grebel, Centre d'Accueil pour Étudiants Étrangers," 15 January 1977, Foyer Grebel Archive, Centre Mennonite de Paris, France.

affairs. The council's first task was to give the center a name. The discussions that followed clarified the group's understanding of the center's purpose. It envisioned a ministry that responded comprehensively to African students' needs, those of both body and soul. By providing students with a temporary place to live and aiding them in the search for permanent housing, the center offered a basic service that existing student organizations and evangelical ministries did not.[96] At the same time, the center's theologically and missiologically Anabaptist orientation demanded that staff share a call to personal faith and to expression of that faith in a community of believers.[97] "For those who come and live in the home," Neal Blough reported, "there will be a Christian presence, something concrete that they will see living and working. When we share our faith, this community will be the expression, although imperfect, of a group that wishes to be faithful disciples of the Lord."[98] The council intended to support the formation of Christian students, encouraging them to return to their countries ready to serve in local churches. Given these objectives, the local committee named the center Foyer Grebel, after the sixteenth-century Anabaptist leader Conrad Grebel. Grebel had studied in Paris, returned to his native country of Switzerland, come to faith, and contributed in significant

Life at Foyer Grebel

ways to the formation of the first Anabaptist congregation in his home country. By this name, the committee concluded, "many will come to know the Evangelical Mennonite Church."[99]

To fulfill its purposes, Foyer Grebel required major renovations, which were carried out slowly as money and labor became available. Related expenses were

96 Larry Miller, "Rapport Moral 1976–77" for Foyer Grebel, 30 August 1977, personal files of Robert Witmer, Cambridge, ON.

97 Neal Blough, interview by David Neufeld, 7 June 2012.

98 Neal Blough, "Le Foyer Grebel," *Christ Seul*, January 1977, 4–7.

99 Tshinabu Tshimika, Minutes of Council of the Foyer in Saint Maurice, 16 October 1976, Foyer Grebel Archive, Centre Mennonite de Paris, France.

shared by MMF and MBM.[100] Participants in several work camps helped remodel the home, saving the project large sums of money and allowing French Mennonites and their congregations to become familiar with the student ministry.[101] While preparations continued, the center's personnel provided material, moral, and spiritual support to students.

The local council delegated the center's "social services" to the Bloughs.[102] The couple's main task was to help orient and settle African students in Paris by mitigating the difficulties they encountered after arriving in the city. This work involved picking students up at the airport, helping them gain access to student supports, inviting them to take up temporary residence at Foyer Grebel, and helping them find permanent housing.[103] The Bloughs' attempts to obtain documentation, housing, and jobs for students introduced the couple to the pervasive racism that Africans in Paris faced.[104] In *Christ Seul*, Neal described his experience

A Foyer Grebel Bible study

100 Larry Miller, Financial Prognosis of Foyer Grebel prepared for EMEK, 17 November 1979. Box 2, Folder 11. Mennonite Board of Missions Overseas Ministry Division Data Files Part 5, 1975–1979. IV/18/013-05. Mennonite Church USA Archives. Goshen, IN.

101 Minutes of the MMF General Assembly, 1 November 1975, photocopy of *Cahier Officiel* of MMF; Larry Miller, "Rapport Moral 1976–77" for Foyer Grebel, 30 August 1977, personal files of Robert Witmer, Cambridge, ON.

102 Tshinabu Tshimika, Minutes of Council of the Foyer in Saint Maurice, 16 October 1976, Foyer Grebel Archive, Centre Mennonite de Paris, France.

103 Neal Blough, "Le Foyer Grebel," *Christ Seul*, January 1977, 4–7.

104 Neal Blough, "Mission in Europe: Reflecting on the Missiological Legacy of Wilbert Shenk," in *Evangelical, Ecumenical, and Anabaptist Missiologies in Conversation: Essays in Honor of Wilbert R. Shenk*, ed. James R. Krabill, Walter Sawatsky, and Charles E. Van Engen (Maryknoll, NY: Orbis, 2006), 220.

of trying to establish a lodging network of apartment owners willing to rent to African students:

> I visited a real estate agency and one of their first questions was whether my friends were white or black. Another agent told me that about 80% of the landlords he worked with told him that they did not want to rent to Africans. After these experiences, I finally found a studio for my friends and, when they arrived, we visited it. After having paid the first month's rent, the building manager told us that we could not invite black or Arab friends to the building.[105]

The Bloughs kept in touch with students who found housing outside of Foyer Grebel, attempting to provide support to them by inviting them to participate in the center's activities.[106]

These activities, which came to include Bible and English classes,[107] were organized and directed by Larry and Eleanor Miller, who were appointed as the center's organizers by the local council.[108] As those responsible for the home's operation, the Millers determined the center's policy on rent and duration of stay. They gave priority to students who had demonstrated difficulty in finding housing and, because there was a particular shortage of apartments for families, offered subsidized rent for married couples.[109] Two rooms would be available for a period of one year, and the rest for three months. Rent would give students access to a common kitchen and laundry facility.[110]

In November 1976, the Millers moved into Foyer Grebel, opening a limited space to welcome residents. Shortly thereafter, the center received its first occupants, a couple from Chad.[111] Within a matter of

---

105 Neal Blough, "Le Foyer Grebel," *Christ Seul*, January 1977, 4–7.

106 Denys Laruelle, Minutes of Foyer Grebel Local Council, 7 May 1977, Foyer Grebel Archive, Centre Mennonite de Paris, France.

107 Minutes of the Executive Council of Foyer Grebel, 5 March 1983, Foyer Grebel Archive, Centre Mennonite de Paris, France.

108 Tshinabu Tshimika, Minutes of Council of the Foyer in Saint Maurice, 16 October 1976, Foyer Grebel Archive, Centre Mennonite de Paris, France.

109 "Foyer Grebel," *Christ Seul*, May 1977, i–iv.

110 Tshinabu Tshimika, Minutes of Foyer Grebel Local Council, 15 January 1977, Foyer Grebel Archive, Centre Mennonite de Paris, France.

111 MMF Report, "Foyer Grebel, Centre d'Accueil pour Étudiants Étrangers," 15 January 1977, Foyer Grebel Archive, Centre Mennonite de Paris, France.

A Sunday outing for the Foyer Grebel Christian Community at Fontainebleau (ca. 1981)

months, twelve single students, two couples, and two babies resided in Foyer Grebel.[112] From this point forward, the Millers spent a significant amount of their time relating to students in the interest of maintaining a healthy community environment. In a time of significant upheaval in francophone Africa, political differences between students were a constant source of tension, but Foyer Grebel remained open to all students who fit the center's requirements.[113]

The Foyer Grebel staff frequently visited French Mennonite congregations in eastern France to familiarize them with the center's purpose and to raise funds. The project was a missionary venture receiving no state subsidies and was therefore dependent on private French funds for its operation.[114] In these visits, the Foyer Grebel North American staff focused on the collaborative nature of the student ministry, hoping to transform the perception that the work in

Christmas program with children, led by Lydia Schultz

Saint Maurice was solely a North American project. Ideally, only members of MMF or the French Mennonite Mission Committee, who accompanied MBM personnel, would appeal for financial support.[115] Initially, Foyer Grebel staff expressed frustration about the difficulty of communicating the pressing needs of

112 Larry and Eléonore Miller, "Nouvelles du Foyer Grebel," *Christ Seul*, August/September 1977, 4.

113 Minutes of Foyer Grebel Local Council, 1 April 1978, Foyer Grebel Archive, Centre Mennonite de Paris, France.

114 Minutes of the MMF General Assembly, 31 October 1976, photocopy of *Cahier Officiel* of MMF, personal files of Robert Witmer, Cambridge, ON.

115 Tshinabu Tshimika, Minutes of Foyer Grebel Local Council, 26 November 1976, Foyer Grebel Archive, Centre Mennonite de Paris, France.

foreign students in Paris to Mennonite congregations far removed from the capital and the challenges of urban life.[116] Over time, however, their visits succeeded in generating broader support for the new ministry.

Foyer Grebel extended an invitation to all French Mennonites to be present at the center's inauguration on September 10, 1977.[117] Coinciding with the MMF annual general assembly, the ceremony was attended by the association's leadership and representatives of MBM and the French Mennonite Mission Committee. The city's mayor opened the festivities in Saint Maurice's community hall, promising that the municipality would provide "all the support required for the smooth functioning of the foyer and for its development." Wilbert Shenk and Pierre Widmer, who still represented the French Mennonite Mission Committee, both emphasized the unique example of international collaboration in missions that was presently expressed in Foyer Grebel. Widmer, justifying his committee's support of the project, told the audience that "we need a new vision that exists outside of the traditional framework

Members of the Châtenay-Malabry congregation watching a slideshow on a Sunday afternoon outing at Foyer Grebel (1977)

of missions." This vision had been provided by Foyer Grebel "missionary work with foreigners who are at our door."[118]

116 Minutes of Foyer Grebel Local Council, 12 March 1978, Foyer Grebel Archive, Centre Mennonite de Paris, France.

117 "Foyer Grebel," *Christ Seul*, August/September 1977, i–iv.

118 M. and R. Peterschmitt, "Inauguration et Dédicace," *Christ Seul*, January 1978, 7–8, 25–26.

Europäisches Mennonitisches Evangelisationskomitee Becomes a Partner in Foyer Grebel

A commitment to mission activity in Europe, which Foyer Grebel embodied, was gaining increasing support among European Mennonite groups outside France that in the past had expressed skepticism about the need for such efforts. In October 1979, representatives of Europäisches Mennonitisches Evangelisationskomitee (EMEK; European Mennonite Missions Committee) visited Foyer Grebel to explore the possibility of supporting its ministry.[119] EMEK had been organized in 1952 to promote and support the mission efforts of Mennonites in Germany, the Netherlands, Switzerland, and France. In 1963, the French Mennonite Mission Committee, which was represented on EMEK's board, had asked the agency to take over administration of the French Mennonite mission in Chad, which had been established in 1953 through the missionary activity of Raymond Eyer.[120] With the closing of this

Children of the Châtenay-Malabry congregation being hosted by staff of Foyer Grebel on a 1977 outing to the center

mission field because of political strife, EMEK saw support of Foyer Grebel as an opportunity to prolong its mission to Africa.[121] The committee expressed its concern that Foyer Grebel not turn into an exclusively

---

119 Jean-Paul Herzog, Minutes of Foyer Grebel Local Council, 20 October 1978, Foyer Grebel Archive, Centre Mennonite de Paris, France.

120 Harold S. Bender and Leo Laurense, "Europäisches Mennonitisches Evangelisationskomitee," *Global Anabaptist*

Mennonite Encyclopedia Online, http://www.gameo.org/encyclopedia/contents/E879.html.

121 Aboh Danrhé, "Note à l'Attention de M. le Préfet," 2 November 1992, Foyer Grebel Archive, Centre Mennonite de Paris, France.

internal mission.[122] However, EMEK acknowledged that its association with the center represented an important relocation and reorientation of its activity.[123]

Foyer Grebel and its sponsors welcomed EMEK's interest. They were excited about the extension of the center's "experiment in inter-Mennonite cooperation,"[124] and were delighted with this manifestation of European Mennonite interest in domestic missions.[125] They viewed EMEK's participation as another concrete bridge of collaboration between European and North American Mennonites.[126] In November 1979, at an agency meeting EMEK approved a motion to support Foyer Grebel. The committee's new role included financial support of the center's operations and the possible posting of non-French European staff to the center in the future.[127]

EMEK's involvement in Foyer Grebel required reorganization of the center's administrative structure. In October 1982, the three parties drafted an "Agreement of Collaboration" that placed EMEK alongside MMF and MBM as an equal partner in the project, exclusive of legal responsibilities that remained under the charge of the French association. The agreement proposed to form an executive council with equal representation for the three organizations and the French Mennonite Mission Committee and with open positions for delegates from an assortment of other interested parties. The council's participants were charged with accurately representing the interests and positions of their respective

122 Minutes of Foyer Grebel Local Council, 25 October 1980, Foyer Grebel Archive, Centre Mennonite de Paris, France.

123 Extract of EMEK Report of 17 November 1979 meeting at the Thomashof, Karlsruhe, translated into French, Foyer Grebel Archive, Centre Mennonite de Paris, France.

124 Neal Blough to Stanley Kauffman, 7 January 1980. Box 4, Folder 19. Mennonite Board of Missions Overseas Ministry Division Data Files Part 6, 1980–1984. IV/18/013-06. Mennonite Church USA Archives. Goshen, IN.

125 Wilbert Shenk to Raymond Eyer, 6 March 1980. Box 4, Folder 19. Mennonite Board of Missions Overseas Ministry Division Data Files Part 6, 1980–1984. IV/18/013-06. Mennonite Church USA Archives. Goshen, IN.

126 "Rapport Moral," Foyer Grebel, 1979–80. Box 4, Folder 19. Mennonite Board of Missions Overseas Ministry Division Data Files Part 6, 1980–1984. IV/18/013-06. Mennonite Church USA Archives. Goshen, IN.

127 E. Kennel, Minutes of Foyer Grebel Local Council, 1 December 1979, Foyer Grebel Archive, Centre Mennonite de Paris, France.

organizations in the determination of the center's general direction, functioning principles, budget, and personnel. The council's decisions would be achieved by consensus to the greatest degree possible.[128] All involved parties immediately approved this agreement. MMF then delegated administrative authority to the newly formed council.[129]

The Early Life of Foyer Grebel

Administrative restructuring did not hinder the everyday functioning of the center. The Foyer Grebel staff convened daily to assign tasks and discuss concerns and met weekly for a worship service and decision-making meeting.[130] Every two weeks, the team organized a Bible study with French Mennonite theological students and members of Foyer Fraternel.[131] The staff's community

life was further enriched through collaboration and dialogue with other evangelical student ministries. In 1977, the official administrative address of the ACEAP, the African student association once staffed by Marlin Miller, moved to Foyer Grebel. This organization played an important role in creating and maintaining

French Mennonite students in Paris, members of the Châtenay-Malabry congregation, and staff of Foyer Grebel sharing a common meal (1978)

128 Text of Agreement of Collaboration, October 1982, Foyer Grebel Archive, Centre Mennonite de Paris, France.

129 Minutes of the Executive Council of Foyer Grebel, 5 March 1983, Foyer Grebel Archive, Centre Mennonite de Paris, France.

130 André and Martha Hege, Minutes of the Executive Council of Foyer Grebel, 9 October 1982, Foyer Grebel Archive, Centre Mennonite de Paris, France.

131 Neal Blough, "Le Foyer Grebel," *Christ Seul*, 4–7.

contacts between the center and churches in Africa.[132] In the same year, Foyer Grebel formed a relationship with the Accueil Fraternel des Étudiants et Stagiaires d'Outre-Mer, a ministry of the Franco-Swiss Protestant Mission to Chad that helped foreign students and trainees adapt to life in France. The two projects, each supported in part by French Mennonite funds, were located in close proximity to each other and shared a common desire to provide liaison services to African students. Their staffs met regularly for prayer.[133]

Foyer Grebel's capacity to respond to the housing needs of students soon grew. In October 1979, the Baptist Church of the Tabernacle offered its Bethanie retirement home, located in the suburb of Saint-Ouen, to MMF for the association's use. The Foyer Grebel local council viewed this offer as a gift from God, and determined to use the facility to extend its existing lodging network. MMF accepted the council's proposal. Steve Johnson, a North American MCC volunteer, led the effort to prepare the building for occupancy. MMF provided loans for the cost of renovations with funds from Service Épargne Mennonite and French Mennonite congregations, and the Mont des Oiseaux children's home donated the furnishings.[134] The local council appointed French Mennonite theological student Claude Baecher as the new center's first part-time director.[135] By October 1980, fourteen foreign students, all recommended by Foyer Grebel, occupied Foyer Bethanie.[136]

Communauté Chrétienne du Foyer Grebel

Notwithstanding the student residence's success, the Foyer Grebel leadership maintained that the integrity of the center's witness depended on the existence of a community of believers closely tied to the lodging

132 Théo Hege, Minutes of Foyer Grebel Local Council, 19 November 1977, Foyer Grebel Archive, Centre Mennonite de Paris, France.

133 A. and M. Fermaud, "L'Acceuil Fraternel,' Christ Seul, January 1977, 1.

134 Robert Witmer, Report on Foyer Bethanie, 16 October 1980. Box 4, Folder 19. Mennonite Board of Missions Overseas Ministry Division Data Files Part 6, 1980–1984. IV/18/013-06. Mennonite Church USA Archives. Goshen, IN; Robert Witmer, "Foyer Bethanie," Christ Seul, January 1981, 36.

135 E. Kennel, Minutes of Foyer Grebel Local Council, 1 December 1979, Foyer Grebel Archive, Centre Mennonite de Paris, France.

136 Robert Witmer, Report on Foyer Bethanie, 16 October 1980. Box 4, Folder 19. Mennonite Board of Missions Overseas Ministry Division Data Files Part 6, 1980–1984. IV/18/013-06. Mennonite Church USA Archives. Goshen, IN

facilities.[137] Now that all the available rooms were filled to capacity, the staff directed their efforts to developing the center's common spiritual life. They extended a call to discipleship to students often struggling to understand their experience in a foreign environment. At this critical juncture in students' lives, they were given a forum in Wednesday night Bible studies and Sunday

Lively worship at Foyer Grebel Christian Community

137 "Rapport Moral," Foyer Grebel, 1979–80. Box 4, Folder 19. Mennonite Board of Missions Overseas Ministry Division Data Files Part 6, 1980–1984. IV/18/013-06. Mennonite Church USA Archives. Goshen, IN.

evening meetings to discuss the challenges of living out their faith in a new place. These gatherings resulted in the birth of a faith community with informal organization but clear goals. In December 1978, the community produced a founding document, which stated,

> Throughout history, for almost two thousand years and again today, a multitude of men and women from all places, cultures, and conditions have responded to God's call and have become a part of God's people. We, members of the Foyer Grebel community, have also heard that call. . . . We recognize in a particular way the work of God in the very presence of the Foyer Grebel. This presence is owed to the common action of American, European and African Christians who share an objective to serve and testify to foreign students. We are from different races, nationalities, and religious traditions, but God has shown us that in Jesus, there is neither African, nor European, nor American any longer, but a new humanity.

"By the grace of God and with the help of the Holy Spirit," the community's members committed to engage in communal Bible study to determine God's will, discern gifts and talents, and deepen faith. They promised to pray for and share with one another, practice mutual aid, follow Jesus's instruction in Matthew 18 in the case of conflict, respect the group's racial and religious diversity, and share the gospel with other students.[138] Joseph and Yolande Yenge, a Baptist couple from Zaire, were asked to serve as part-time ministers to the group of fifteen regular participants. The establishment of Communauté Chrétienne du Foyer Grebel (CCFG) represented the most significant accomplishment of the center's ministry, Larry Miller believed.[139]

While in Paris in 1980, Wilbert Shenk encouraged the community to consider becoming a church. In an October retreat, the group began a process of discernment to consider future directions. Discussion surrounded a number of questions: What basic elements of a church did the existing community lack? Could a community made up of transient foreigners become a faithful church? In a community that integrated a variety of confessional traditions, what tendency or

denominational identity would be adopted? The answers to these questions were not immediately evident. CCFG held Bible studies on the issues of baptism, the Lord's Supper, and worship, often consulting with members of Foyer Fraternel or MMF.[140] The clear result of this process was the community's determination to become a church.[141]

On a Sunday morning in February 1982, the group of twenty believers shared communion together for the first time.[142] Church members soon took on roles as Bible teachers, or as deacons who administered the community's funds. CCFG members called Neal Blough to serve as the group's "shepherd," a role that incorporated spiritual guidance, outreach, and coordination of activities.[143] With the encouragement of the Foyer Grebel local council and MMF, the congregation continued to deliberate over its denominational iden-

138 Founding document of the Communauté Chrétienne du Foyer Grebel, December 1978, Foyer Grebel Archive, Centre Mennonite de Paris, France.

139 Larry Miller, "Rapport Moral," Foyer Grebel, 1977–78. Box 2, Folder 11. Mennonite Board of Missions Overseas Ministry Division Data Files Part 5, 1975–1979. IV/18/013-05. Mennonite Church USA Archives. Goshen, IN.

140 Neal Blough, interview by David Neufeld, 7 June 2012.

141 Foyer Grebel Annual Report 1980–81, 1 April 1982, Foyer Grebel Archive, Centre Mennonite de Paris, France.

142 Ibid.

143 André and Martha Hege, Minutes of the Executive Council of Foyer Grebel, 9 October 1982, Foyer Grebel Archive, Centre Mennonite de Paris, France.

tity.[144] "Should the church become Mennonite simply to reflect the beliefs of the center's staff, especially when the majority of France's Mennonites lived so far away?" the group wondered.[145] A lack of consensus left this issue temporarily unresolved. Nevertheless, CCFG celebrated the confessional and racial diversity of its community through which, in Blough's words, "some of the barriers that separate cultures, races and nations are broken down through Jesus Christ and the good News of reconciliation becomes a visible reality."[146]

From the time of the center's birth, Foyer Grebel's supervising organizations had sought out a French missionary couple to take over the direction of the project from the Millers. Ongoing fundraising tours to Mennonite churches by Foyer Grebel staff were accompanied by calls to service in the center. Despite the emergence of several candidates, the search was initially unsuccessful. Nevertheless, EMEK funds opened

the possibility of the formation of a more culturally diverse staff. Starting in 1980, the agency supported a part-time administrative assistant position filled by French Mennonite Elisabeth Baecher.[147] One year later, EMEK paid for the salaries of Jakob and Hotsche Kikkert, a Dutch Mennonite couple who participated in the center's work over a period of several years.[148] Finally, in 1982, the French couple Denis and Lydia Schultz agreed to accept a call to serve as directors of Foyer Grebel. This personnel change conformed to the established model of the transfer of control of MBM-initiated programs into French hands. Several years earlier, MBM had committed itself to purchase an apartment down the street from the center, in part to ensure "permanent collaboration" between a North American couple and the new directors.[149] From this location, the

144 Minutes of Foyer Grebel Local Council, 25 October 1980, Foyer Grebel Archive, Centre Mennonite de Paris, France.

145 Blough, "Mission in Europe," 220.

146 Neal Blough to Stanley Kauffman, 7 January 1980. Box 4, Folder 19. Mennonite Board of Missions Overseas Ministry Division Data Files Part 6, 1980–1984. IV/18/013-06. Mennonite Church USA Archives. Goshen, IN.

147 E. Kennel, Minutes of Foyer Grebel Local Council, 1 December 1979, Foyer Grebel Archive, Centre Mennonite de Paris, France.

148 E. Kennel, Minutes of Foyer Grebel Local Council, 17 October 1981, Foyer Grebel Archive, Centre Mennonite de Paris, France.

149 E. Peterschmitt, Minutes of Foyer Grebel Local Council, 2 December 1978, Foyer Grebel Archive, Centre Mennonite de Paris, France.

Bloughs continued to participate in and support the life of Foyer Grebel and CCFG.

Financial Support for Evangelistic Ventures, 1977–82

Support for Evangelistic Media

The arrival of the Schultzes set Foyer Grebel's future on firm foundations. Its sponsoring partners were able to pursue other cooperative initiatives from a position of strength and confidence. These efforts included financial support for evangelistic publication and broadcasting activities. In 1977, Robert Witmer became aware of MBM Media Ministry's publication of the Mennonite Faith Series, a four-volume collection authored by J. C. Wenger "intended to set forth the principle points of Mennonite history, faith, life and activity as well as their 'Mennonite' relations to other Christians."[150] Witmer hoped to provide these resources to French Mennonites in translation. The MMF leadership supported the project but did not have

European Mennonite Evangelism Committee (EMEK) financially supported a Dutch Mennonite couple, Hotsche and Jakob Kikkert, for an assignment at Foyer Grebel lasting several years.

space or personnel to launch a publishing venture and was concerned about a lack of readership. In conversations with Pierre Widmer, then still editor of *Christ Seul*, Witmer proposed to publish the volumes as a series of *cahiers* (notebooks) to be offered to subscribers of the French monthly as a trimestral supplement.[151] In

150 Larry Miller, "Annual Report," MBM in France, 21 October 1980. Box 4, Folder 19. Mennonite Board of Missions Overseas Ministry Division Data Files Part 6, 1980–1984. IV/18/013-06. Mennonite Church USA Archives. Goshen, IN.

151 Robert Witmer to Pierre Lugbull, 23 April 2001, personal files of Robert Witmer, Cambridge, ON.

this way, the material would be made available more easily to two thousand French Mennonite homes. Widmer and MMF favored Witmer's plan. They offered to cover the series' publication expenses, while MBM paid the copyright and translating fees. Wenger's brochures were printed by the French Baptist press in Massy. In the July 1980 issue, Pierre Sommer announced the start of *Christ Seul*'s cahiers series.[152]

Two years later, MMF approved the further dissemination of MBM evangelistic media content in France, this time in the form of radio programs.[153] MBM had sought French Mennonite institutional support for its radio broadcasts as early as 1969, but it was not until 1982 that MMF and MBM engaged in fruitful discussions on the topic.[154] After consulting with the French Mennonite conference, the two partners signed a contract with an evangelical broadcaster in Mulhouse, and the broadcast of MBM programs in translation began soon afterward.[155]

Financial Support for Mission Work in Quintanadueñas, Spain

In 1982, MMF extended its financial support of evangelistic work in Europe by approving a donation to the Mennonite mission in Quintanadueñas, a small community just north of Burgos in Spain.[156] In 1978, José Gallardo, who had pastored a Mennonite church in Belgium, helped found a Christian community in the village; it served as a center for the rehabilitation of marginalized youth and their families. Three years later, MBM bolstered this ministry by sending missionaries Dennis and Connie Byler to collaborate with Gallardo and the community's members. Soon thereafter, MMF representatives Ernest Nussbaumer, André Pelsy, Willy Muller, and Robert Witmer visited the community, returning to the MMF administrative council with a

152 Pierre Sommer, "Mission Mennonite Française," *Christ Seul*, July 1980, 14.

153 Pierre Sommer, "Les Réunions de la Mission Mennonite Française," *Christ Seul*, June 1982, 7–8.

154 Robert Witmer to Kenneth J. Weaver, 27 June 1969. Mennonite Board of Missions Overseas Ministry Division Data Files Part 3, 1966–1969. IV/18/013-03. Mennonite Church USA Archives. Goshen, IN.

155 "Proposition de Contrat entre le MBM-la MMF-le CDEM," undated. Mennonite Board of Missions Overseas Ministry Division Data Files Part 6, 1980–1984. IV/18/013-06. Mennonite Church USA Archives. Goshen, IN.

156 G.-W. Muller, "Assemblée Générale de la Mission Mennonite Française," *Christ Seul*, June 1982, 6.

recommendation to financially support the extension of the Burgos mission to Brieva, an abandoned mining town east of the city.[157] The Quintanadueñas community had run out of living space, and the proposed extension of the Spanish mission's work was vital to its capacity to spread its service and witness to new people. The MMF general assembly agreed to support this expansion, appealing to French Mennonites to fund the effort through Service Épargne Mennonite.[158]

The Therapeutic Village at Verrières-le-Buisson, 1975–85

A Response to Social and Spiritual Needs

The last significant branch of the partners' evangelistic activity grew out of Lois and Robert Witmer's work in Verrières-le-Buisson. The couple had moved to the Paris suburb in 1975, occupying a home built by

MCC Pax volunteers on a lot purchased by MMF.[159] Following their withdrawal from full-time ministry

In 1974 the Pax team built the last of five identical Canadian houses. This one, in Verrières-le-Buisson, became home to Robert and Lois Witmer (pictured on the right) and their family.

157 Pierre Sommer, "Les Réunions de la Mission Mennonite Française," *Christ Seul*, 7–8.

158 SEM Fundraising Appeal, undated, MBM Archive. Mennonite Board of Missions Overseas Ministry Division Data Files Part 6, 1980–1984. IV/18/013-06. Mennonite Church USA Archives. Goshen, IN.

159 Robert Witmer, Summary of Origin and Stewardship of Funds and Development of Investments in Partnership Programs from 1954 to 1983, personal files of Robert Witmer, Cambridge, ON.

at Foyer Fraternel, the Witmers had expressed readiness to devote themselves again to church planting and evangelism.[160] While pursuing these goals, they came into contact with a number of individuals who had experienced spiritual renewal in the Catholic charismatic movement. Unexpectedly, one Catholic sister asked the Witmers to lead a small group of believers who had been meeting in her apartment for Bible study and prayer.[161] Beginning in September 1977, the Witmers held regular meetings in the basement of Foyer Fraternel, which were often attended by a local priest. Before long, several members of this interconfessional group began participating actively in the Mennonite congregation.[162]

Through their new Catholic contacts, the Witmers developed a relationship with Michel and Françoise Augris, with whom they shared a common interest in

One of the interconfessional (mostly Catholic) Bible study–praise and prayer fellowship groups that gathered in the Witmer home regularly from 1975 to early 1984

caring for people with acute social and spiritual needs.[163] In their work, both couples frequently encountered fragile and broken households and individuals suffering

160 Wilbert Shenk, "Administrative Visit Report, France, February 21–23," 20 March 1975. Box 2, Folder 11. Mennonite Board of Missions Overseas Ministry Division Data Files Part 5, 1975–1979. IV/18/013-05. Mennonite Church USA Archives. Goshen, IN.

161 Robert Witmer, e-mail message to author, 5 October 2012.

162 Robert Witmer to Wilbert Shenk, 12 October 1977. Box 2, Folder 11. Mennonite Board of Missions Overseas Ministry

Division Data Files Part 5, 1975–1979. IV/18/013-05. Mennonite Church USA Archives. Goshen, IN; Robert Witmer, "Struggles of Faith and Life in a Paris Suburb," 6 March 1978, personal files of Robert Witmer, Cambridge, ON.

163 Neal Blough, "Annual Report," MBM in France, 29 October 1981. Box 4, Folder 19. Mennonite Board of Missions Overseas Ministry Division Data Files Part 6, 1980–1984. IV/18/013-06. Mennonite Church USA Archives. Goshen, IN.

from debilitating health issues. They were impressed by the pervasive loneliness that characterized their social environment. In the estimation of Robert and Lois Witmer and Michel and Françoise Augris, many members of the community were in need of more than a typical relationship to a church. They felt a call to seek a solution to this problem "on a semi-communitarian basis."[164] They proposed the creation of a "therapeutic village" where an interconfessional group of committed believers would welcome and provide care to needy individuals in a loving and supportive Christian environment.[165] They hoped to root the community's spiritual life in Foyer Fraternel.

Diverse Reactions to the Therapeutic Village Project

MMF administrators gave Witmer significant leeway to develop this vision. MBM's support for the project was also steady. "We believe it is one way of communicating the gospel to people who live in societies where traditional structures of family and community life are being eroded and people are searching for healing and wholeness in community," Shenk affirmed.[166] Among Foyer Fraternel's membership, support for the project was mixed, even after a series of Bible studies and discussions were convened to discuss the project.[167] Certainly, some viewed the presence of Catholic charismatics in the congregation's life as a positive contribution to its diversity. In *Christ Seul*, Claude Baecher reported that the participation of individuals from "'charismatic' groups, the workshop, Foyer Grebel, the village ministry, Mennonites from the east, Americans, Parisians, MMF, Foyer Fraternel, [and] Nogent . . . allows us to appreciate the diversity within our unity, because we complement one another." "This variety," he continued, "is not only complementary, but is also a way of evidencing the gospel of Jesus Christ." Furthermore, with regards to the therapeutic village, he stated that "the members of the congregation believe in this

---

164 Robert Witmer, "France: Annual Report, 1978," December 1978, personal files of Robert Witmer, Cambridge, ON.

165 Jean Hassenforder, "La Contribution Mennonite au Développement de Témoins," 27 July 2000, personal files of Robert Witmer, Cambridge, ON.

166 Wilbert Shenk to Neal Blough, 27 September 1979. Box 2, Folder 11. Mennonite Board of Missions Overseas Ministry Division Data Files Part 5, 1975–1979. IV/18/013-05. Mennonite Church USA Archives. Goshen, IN.

167 Neal Blough to Wilbert Shenk, 14 June 1979, personal files of Robert Witmer, Cambridge, ON.

Four interconfessional groups met together each month in the Châtenay-Malabry Mennonite Church, where they increasingly felt at home.

form of evangelism more than . . . a more aggressive encroachment on the public square."[168]

But an important segment of the congregation expressed hesitation about the village. Because of their previous experience with the workshop, many were familiar with the difficulties of maintaining a healthy and

mutually enriching relationship between the congregation and a new project. In a June 1979 letter intended for MMF and MBM administrators, they shared a number of concerns. Fundamentally, the congregation recognized that the proposed ministry had a strong biblical basis and responded to real needs. Its members believed that the development of the project could be favorable to the congregation. However, they wished to clarify that Foyer Fraternel was not in a position to assume sole responsibility for the venture, especially given ongoing concerns surrounding the church's leadership following the Witmers' departure. In their minds, the resolution of this uncertainty was a necessary precursor to the launching of a new project. Therefore, they argued, "the responsibility for the village should be defined and shared together by the concerned parties: village, congregation, MMF, MBM. Decisions concerning the village [must] be taken together." Finally, they sought reassurance that village staff and participants would be encouraged to integrate into the life of the congregation, and that the village's internal activities would not impede this from occurring. Foyer Fraternel voiced these concerns in the hope that they would be considered by MMF and MBM in their discussions

---

168 Claude Baecher, "Châtenay-Malabry," *Christ Seul*, January 1981, 8.

about the village's future. Despite their hesitations, the membership expressed their approval of the Verrières ministry.[169]

MBM interpreted the Foyer Fraternel letter as an appeal to restructure the village project's supervisory framework. Although directly impacted by the ministry's development, the congregation had felt excluded from decision-making processes, the mission board observed. Furthermore, it was clear that Witmer's dual role as MMF executive secretary and village project director was becoming increasingly awkward. Pierre Widmer's departure from MMF and the French association's unwillingness or inability to accept Witmer's resignation led to the concentration of responsibility and power in his and, thereby, MBM's hands.[170] As a result, the partnership's existing administrative configuration inhibited the practice of mutual accountability to a significant degree.[171] Despite their recognition of the need for supervisory restructuring, MBM administrators, being farthest from the scene, were not interested in taking a leadership role in initiating this process. Thus, they eagerly endorsed MMF's creation of a local management and supervisory committee that would include representatives of the French association, MBM, and Foyer Fraternel.[172] Any significant development or change of orientation for the project would be submitted to this committee for approval.[173]

The concerns that emerged in the study commission's discussions were primarily related to the new project's relationship to Foyer Fraternel. How would the village ensure that its activities did not interfere with those of the congregation? What steps would it take to inhibit divisions along confessional lines and to encourage the complete and healthy integration of

169 Neal Blough to Wilbert Shenk, 14 June 1979, personal files of Robert Witmer, Cambridge, ON.

170 Wilbert Shenk to Robert Witmer, 19 July 1979. Box 5, Folder 12. Mennonite Board of Missions Overseas Ministry Division Data Files Part 5, 1975–1979. IV/18/013-05. Mennonite Church USA Archives. Goshen, IN.

171 Neal Blough to Wilbert Shenk, 14 June 1979, personal files of Robert Witmer, Cambridge, ON.

172 Wilbert Shenk to Neal Blough, 27 September 1979. Box 5, Folder 12. Mennonite Board of Missions Overseas Ministry Division Data Files Part 5, 1975–1979. IV/18/013-05. Mennonite Church USA Archives. Goshen, IN.

173 Robert Witmer to Wilbert Shenk, 3 July 1979, personal files of Robert Witmer, Cambridge, ON.

its Catholic members into the congregation? What strains would the community's operation place on the congregation's resources? As a first step toward addressing these concerns, the commission asked the village's leadership to provide a written description of the group's basic doctrinal positions and an explanation of its central goals.[174]

The Witmers, leaders of the Foyer Fraternel interconfessional study group and visionaries and directors of the now-functioning village, were aware of these concerns. In a letter to Shenk, they explained that they had "lived with the tension between conviction and objection regarding this village project" since its outset. While the couple had received strong affirmation for the work from a variety of institutional sources and understood their work as proceeding under "the leading and blessing of the Lord," they recognized the existence of persistent "uneasiness" and "fear" surrounding the village's development. In light of these circumstances, they sought a definitive determination concerning the project's future.[175] Shenk, while maintaining that MBM believed that the concept was "too good not to be implemented,"[176] encouraged the missionaries to continue to listen to the various partners' concerns with patience, noting that "innovation is seldom accepted without pain or apprehension."[177]

In this atmosphere of uncertainty, the village community's work carried on. In the spring of 1981, four Canadian volunteers began to prepare the foundations for the construction of a second residence on the MMF land in Verrières, a project the association had approved in 1979 and which represented a significant physical expansion of the village program. On its

---

174 Report of the Study Commission for the Verrières Community Village, undated. Box 2, Folder 11. Mennonite Board of Missions Overseas Ministry Division Data Files Part 5, 1975–1979. IV/18/013-05. Mennonite Church USA Archives. Goshen, IN.

175 Robert Witmer to Wilbert Shenk, 8 July 1981. Box 10, Folder 33. Mennonite Board of Missions Overseas Ministry Division Data Files Part 6, 1980–1984. IV/18/013-06. Mennonite Church USA Archives. Goshen, IN.

176 Wilbert Shenk to Robert Witmer, 11 May 1981. Box 10, Folder 33. Mennonite Board of Missions Overseas Ministry Division Data Files Part 6, 1980–1984. IV/18/013-06. Mennonite Church USA Archives. Goshen, IN.

177 Wilbert Shenk to Robert Witmer, 16 July 1981. Box 10, Folder 33. Mennonite Board of Missions Overseas Ministry Division Data Files Part 6, 1980–1984. IV/18/013-06. Mennonite Church USA Archives. Goshen, IN.

completion, this building was occupied by Michel and Françoise Augris, who had since joined Foyer Fraternel and committed themselves to full-time work in the community's ministry.[178]

Despite this development, the question whether MMF and MBM planned to become more deeply engaged in the project's supervision and direction remained largely unanswered. MMF acceptance of Witmer's resignation as executive secretary at its June 1982 administrative gathering represented a step toward resolving this issue. In light of Witmer's upcoming departure, to be made effective starting July 1983, the MMF administrative council recommended that all interested parties engage in a discussion about the missionary couple's future call. The fact that MMF did not transmit this suggestion directly to MBM administrators demonstrated the limitations that had emerged in

the partners' communication structure.[179] MBM's desire to refrain from managing the MMF administrative decision-making processes meant that it contributed its input exclusively through its own representatives. Thus, the board's primary channel of contact with MMF had almost always been the French association's executive secretary—since 1958, Robert Witmer.[180] For the most part, this arrangement had worked productively. However, in discussions of the Witmers' work at Verrières, it made open communication difficult. MMF saw Witmer and MBM as fathers of the Paris mission and its projects. Its leadership was not willing to broach the subject of the North American couple's future assignment openly, even though this determination fell under their administrative prerogative.[181]

178 Elroy Wideman, "31 Years Ago! Voluntary Service in France (1981)," *Life Together*, Saint Jacobs Mennonite Church, Fall 2012, 10–11; and Neal Blough, "Annual Report," MBM in France, 29 October 1981. Box 4, Folder 19. Mennonite Board of Missions Overseas Ministry Division Data Files Part 6, 1980–1984. IV/18/013-06. Mennonite Church USA Archives. Goshen, IN.

179 Larry Miller to Wilbert Shenk, 29 October 1982. Box 4, Folder 19. Mennonite Board of Missions Overseas Ministry Division Data Files Part 6, 1980–1984. IV/18/013-06. Mennonite Church USA Archives. Goshen, IN.

180 Wilbert Shenk, interview by David Neufeld, 25 July 2011.

181 Wilbert Shenk to Robert Witmer, 26 November 1982. Box 4, Folder 19. Mennonite Board of Missions Overseas Ministry Division Data Files Part 6, 1980–1984. IV/18/013-06. Mennonite Church USA Archives. Goshen, IN.

The decision-making processes dealing with the Witmers' future call and their work in Verrières were further complicated by a conflict that emerged concurrently at Foyer Fraternel over the issue of the discernment of elders. The resulting dispute revealed tensions arising from the interlocking responsibilities of the leadership of the congregation, MMF, and Les Amis de l'Atelier, whose personnel and facilities remained closely linked to the life of Foyer Fraternel. While this proximity had often been mutually enriching and modeled the partners' institutional effort to share the gospel in word and deed, it now aggravated existing differences between key personalities and contributed to mistrust among various parties involved in the partners' work in Châtenay-Malabry.

Partners' Actions Bring
the Therapeutic Village Project to an End

After becoming aware of these dynamics, MBM administrators decided to treat the MMF "unofficial and indirect" recommendation as a "clear appeal" for the board to initiate a review of the Witmers' assignment at Verrières and Châtenay-Malabry.[182] This deliberation formed part of a broader assessment of MBM's mission goals in Paris and in France generally, and a consideration of the future of its partnership with MMF, which was continuing in a period of leadership transition. MBM's review sought to address enduring hesitations about the therapeutic village, which the multiparty supervisory council had failed to address, by exploring how the ministry fit into common MBM, MMF, and congregational objectives. MBM administrators hoped that the review process would conclude with MMF assuming full responsibility for future program direction. Larry Miller—who at the Witmers' request had adopted a mediating role between the community, Foyer Fraternel, and MMF—asked Shenk to plan a visit in spring 1983 to seek a mutually acceptable solution to these ongoing issues.[183]

In an intense series of meetings in March, Shenk met with MBM personnel, members of the MMF administrative council, participants in the village and interconfessional group, and members of Foyer Fraternel. His

---

182 Larry Miller to Wilbert Shenk, 29 October 1982 and Wilbert Shenk to Robert Witmer, 26 November 1982. Box 4,

Folder 19. Mennonite Board of Missions Overseas Ministry Division Data Files Part 6, 1980–1984. IV/18/013-06. Mennonite Church USA Archives. Goshen, IN.

183 Ibid.

resulting determination was clear. MBM's role in the Paris area was to plant churches, and Verrières was not an appropriate location for a new Mennonite church. Furthermore, given Foyer Fraternel's maturity as an independent congregation, and given the persistent if uneven local opposition to the Verrières project, Shenk believed the time had come for the Witmers to enter the final stage of their missionary assignment and prepare to begin work elsewhere.[184] The board's decision adhered to its program principles and policy guidelines.[185] It privileged the preferences of its partners in an attempt to protect the existing fruits of the partnership's past efforts while leaving open the possibility for future collaboration.[186]

This judgment did not meet with universal acceptance. A sector of the congregation continued to support the Witmers' new ministry to an interconfessional community in Verrières. Some expressed concern about the departure of the Witmers and their moderating influence between charismatic and non-charismatic groups in the church.[187] Robert Witmer himself described MBM's decision as an "irredeemable error."[188] His disappointment with the discernment process itself was compounded by an enduring belief in the validity of the interconfessional model the therapeutic village exemplified.[189] He believed MBM's decision had extinguished the experiment's great potential. Nevertheless,

184 "Letter of Information to the Congregation," 18 March 1983, translated by Robert Witmer. Box 10, Folder 33. Mennonite Board of Missions Overseas Ministry Division Data Files Part 6, 1980–1984. IV/18/013-06. Mennonite Church USA Archives. Goshen, IN.

185 Wilbert Shenk to Larry Miller, 20 April 1983. Box 4, Folder 19. Mennonite Board of Missions Overseas Ministry Division Data Files Part 6, 1980–1984. IV/18/013-06. Mennonite Church USA Archives. Goshen, IN.

186 Wilbert Shenk, interviewed by David Neufeld, 25 July 2011.

187 Anne Comtesse to Wilbert Shenk, 26 April 1983. Box 4, Folder 19. Mennonite Board of Missions Overseas Ministry Division Data Files Part 6, 1980–1984. IV/18/013-06. Mennonite Church USA Archives. Goshen, IN.

188 Robert Witmer to Wilbert Shenk and Larry Miller, 2 May 1983. Box 4. Mennonite Board of Missions Overseas Ministry Division Data Files Part 6, 1980–1984. IV/18/013-06. Mennonite Church USA Archives. Goshen, IN.

189 Robert Witmer to Wilbert Shenk, 9 May 1983. Box 10, Folder 33. Mennonite Board of Missions Overseas Ministry Division Data Files Part 6, 1980–1984. IV/18/013-06. Mennonite Church USA Archives. Goshen, IN.

based on MBM's determination, the Witmers agreed to begin a period of transition. They would enter a period of "self-directed study and reflection" in the fall of 1983, during which they would deliberately begin to disengage from the life of Foyer Fraternel.[190] In the summer of 1984, they would end their participation in the congregation and the therapeutic village, which would remain under MMF and MBM supervision.[191]

During this period, MBM asked the Witmers to search for a location for a new missionary effort in the Paris area some distance from the Châtenay-Malabry and Verrières communities.[192] In an October meet-

190 Record of Discussions between Robert and Lois Witmer, Larry Miller and Wilbert Shenk, 14 July 1983. Box 10, Folder 33. Mennonite Board of Missions Overseas Ministry Division Data Files Part 6, 1980–1984. IV/18/013-06. Mennonite Church USA Archives. Goshen, IN.

191 Proposal Concerning the Future of the Verrières Village, the Augris Family, and for Robert and Lois Witmer, undated. Box 4, Folder 19. Mennonite Board of Missions Overseas Ministry Division Data Files Part 6, 1980–1984. IV/18/013-06. Mennonite Church USA Archives. Goshen, IN.

192 Memorandum, Larry Miller to Wilbert Shenk, 7 November 1983. Box 4, Folder 19. Mennonite Board of Missions Overseas Ministry Division Data Files Part 6, 1980–1984. IV/18/013-06. Mennonite Church USA Archives. Goshen, IN.

ing, MBM personnel, including Robert, sketched out a profile of what the couple's future assignment might look like, a document that was shared with MMF and Foyer Fraternel. The group's vision reflected the successful elements of the Verrières project. Its participants envisaged the formation of a community that incorporated a therapeutic village and house church led by missionaries from the Anabaptist Mennonite tradition but serving an interconfessional constituency. The project would require facilities to host individuals who would receive social and spiritual care. The contributors also wished to provide space for a retreat and conference center for interconfessional groups that would observe Anabaptist ministry in action and come into contact with Anabaptist educational resources. In support of this goal, the group proposed to create an Anabaptist Mennonite research and information center, including a reference library.[193]

In December, Robert Witmer submitted a proposal to MBM to purchase a property from the Catholic Foreign Missions Society in Bièvres. The facilities were

193 Robert Witmer, "In Search of a New Mission Location in the Paris Area," 7 December 1983, personal files of Robert Witmer, Cambridge, ON.

ample and, in addition to providing space for the ministries the board's personnel had envisioned, presented an opportunity to establish a "Christian hostel" that might provide income for the community and extend its outreach.[194] MBM was excited about the proposition. However, they wished to proceed cautiously, again not wishing to jeopardize existing relationships and programs. MMF and Foyer Fraternel were both struggling to reformulate new roles in the context of uncertain circumstances. Nevertheless, Shenk wrote, "MBM has taken the position that we are ready to engage on the cutting edge of mission and renewal even though the French Mennonite constituency may not be ready initially to participate; but we would hope that they would at least give us the freedom to move ahead without breaking our ties of relationship."[195]

Even as the Bièvres property was sold to another buyer, the Witmers retained hope that MBM's French partners would support the general proposal. They believed that, as with other partnership ventures, the project could take the form of a nonprofit association tied to MMF, which would continue to provide the legal and spiritual framework for North American work in France and serve as a liaison to French Mennonites.[196] This desire appeared to find expression in MMF approval of a new mission location in Seine-Port, a small town fifty kilometers south of Paris. Although Witmer's second proposal was less ambitious than the Bièvres plan, the program possibilities on the site resembled those of the MBM's initial profile sketch.[197] Having received the go-ahead from both MMF and MBM, Witmer signed a pre-purchase agreement with the property's owners. However, in June 1984, negotiations for the Seine-Port facilities were suspended indefinitely because of a conflict among the property's heirs.[198] The unsuccessful conclusion to the search

194 Robert Witmer, "In Search of a New Mission Location in the Paris Area," 7 December 1983, personal files of Robert Witmer, Cambridge, ON.

195 Wilbert Shenk to Robert Witmer, 23 December 1983, personal files of Robert Witmer, Cambridge, ON.

196 Robert Witmer to Wilbert Shenk, 18 January 1984, personal files of Robert Witmer, Cambridge, ON.

197 Robert Witmer, "In Continued Search of a New Mission Location in the Greater Paris Area," 29 February 1984. Box 4, Folder 19. Mennonite Board of Missions Overseas Ministry Division Data Files Part 6, 1980–1984. IV/18/013-06. Mennonite Church USA Archives. Goshen, IN.

198 Robert Witmer to Wilbert Shenk, 27 June 1984. Box 4, Folder 21. Mennonite Board of Missions Overseas Ministry

for a new mission location coincided with the conclusion of the Witmers' assignment in Verrières and Châtenay-Malabry. In July, after a small celebration, they left France on furlough.[199] They did not return as MBM missionaries. By 1985, MMF had defined no new assignment for the Witmers in France. In MBM's eyes, such an assignment would have been a necessary condition for the couple's redeployment in the country.[200] Instead, the board called them to a church-planting assignment in Rouyn-Noranda, Québec.

The breakdown of the village project and the manner of the Witmers' departure from France injected a degree of uncertainty into the partnership between MMF and MBM, which had experienced significant maturation and growth over the previous decades. MBM remained committed to a joint ministry with MMF in France but had no interest in adopting responsibility for its management or direction. The board wished to enter a new phase of ministry in the country but was unclear about whether its personnel's gifts and vision were understood or supported by French Mennonites.[201] "Does MMF still represent this constituency?" they wondered.[202] MMF, for its part, had experienced a series of disruptive personnel changes that had resulted in administrative strife. It wished to take steps to clarify its orientation as an association and its relationship to MBM in ways that were "missiologically sound."[203] It became clear to both partners that events had provided an opening to renegotiate expectations and to establish new patterns of relating.

Division Data Files Part 6, 1980–1984. IV/18/013-06. Mennonite Church USA Archives. Goshen, IN.

199 André Gaudillere, "Assemblée de Châtenay-Malabry," *Christ Seul*, January 1985, 13–14.

200 Wilbert Shenk, interview by David Neufeld, 25 July 2011.

201 Record of Discussions between Robert and Lois Witmer, Larry Miller, and Wilbert Shenk, 14 July 1983. Box 10, Folder 33. Mennonite Board of Missions Overseas Ministry Division Data Files Part 6, 1980–1984. IV/18/013-06. Mennonite Church USA Archives. Goshen, IN.

202 Robert Witmer to Wilbert Shenk, 25 October 1984. Box 4, Folder 22. Mennonite Board of Missions Overseas Ministry Division Data Files Part 6, 1980–1984. IV/18/013-06. Mennonite Church USA Archives. Goshen, IN.

203 Wilbert Shenk to Neal Blough and Robert Witmer, 19 April 1984. Box 4, Folder 19. Mennonite Board of Missions Overseas Ministry Division Data Files Part 6, 1980–1984. IV/18/013-06. Mennonite Church USA Archives. Goshen, IN.

4
"We Do Not Do the Same Things"
Partnership Comes to an End, 1984–2003

A New Framework for Partnership, 1984-86

Not long after Robert Witmer's resignation as executive secretary of Mission Mennonite Française, representatives of MMF and Mennonite Board of Missions initiated a new round of conversations about the future of their partnership. In these discussions, they considered a number of fundamental issues. How would responsibility for existing ministries be delegated? What structures would guarantee clear and continual communication? Where did the organizations' objectives intersect, and where did they diverge? How could each of the partners' joint projects be integrated more fully into the life of the French Mennonite church? The answers to these questions emerged gradually over the next two decades. As MMF and MBM established new objectives and discerned their identities in response to changing conditions, the ties that bound the partners together weakened. The organizations developed interests in diverging areas of activity, which progressively led them apart. The final outcome of the partners' renegotiation of their relationship was the conclusion of a nearly fifty-year partnership in mission.

This process of recalibration found initial expression in a modified protocol of understanding, drafted by representatives of both organizations in October 1984. This framework laid out the conditions for the partnership's future development. At its heart was a reassertion of the two partners' continuing affinity and their desire "to work together and to help one another in accordance with evangelical Mennonite thought."[1] Both parties remained convinced that the model of intercultural cooperation in mission that they sought to implement gave unique witness to the gospel's unifying power. However, the protocol signaled the beginning of a new stage for the partnership, altering the old framework of collaboration in two important ways.[2] First, its authors formally acknowledged that, for the first time in MMF history, an MBM representative would not occupy the association's executive secretary role. In the past, this position had served as a vital bridge between the two organizations. Beginning in 1954, Orley Swartzentruber and then Robert Witmer had promoted the common interests of both partners, ensuring close consultation and communication between MMF and MBM in the development of programming. Furthermore, the position had safeguarded

the partners' official decision-making structure. While MBM contributed personnel and expressed its desires through them, the onus for final determinations lay with the MMF executive council, to which the North American missionaries were ultimately responsible. Robert and Lois Witmer's departure meant that, from this point forward, French personnel would occupy this key position. While both parties saw this as a healthy development, they needed to create a new mechanism to guarantee future communication and consultation. Thus, MBM committed itself to naming a representative to serve permanently on the MMF executive council.[3]

The second significant change in expectations concerned the relationship's exclusivity. The new document left room for both MMF and MBM to pursue their respective interests without the same degree of mutual dependency that had characterized the partnership since the time of its founding. The protocol no longer demanded that MMF serve as the sole partner for MBM work in France. In keeping with existing understandings, the framework envisioned the establishment of joint MMF and MBM projects in which North

---

1 Larry Miller to Overseas Ministries Division Committee, Attachment, "Protocol of Understanding between the Mennonite Board of Missions (MBM) and the Mission Mennonite Française (MMF)," 21 January 1986. Box 2, Folder 28. Mennonite Board of Missions Overseas Ministry Division Data Files Part 7, 1985–1990. IV/18/013-07. Mennonite Church USA Archives. Goshen, IN.

2 Ibid.

3 Ibid.

American workers would serve under the supervision of the French association, but it also allowed MBM to partner with other French organizations. The board would inform MMF of these activities, but the French association would have no legal or financial responsibility for them. In other words, MBM was no longer required to carry out its work in France exclusively under the auspices of MMF.

This latter modification to the partnership's conditions was motivated by a number of factors. To a great degree, it reflected the MMF leadership's view that the association had "reached its size limit."[4] During the 1960s and '70s, programming had undergone rapid growth. The MMF daughter agencies—Foyer Fraternel, Les Amis de l'Atelier, Domaine Emmanuel, and Foyer Grebel—all stood on firm footing with local administrative bodies assuming responsibility for each project's operation.[5] But the success of these programs stood in contrast with MMF's inability to attain administrative stability or to develop clear connections between its projects and French Mennonite congregations. Thus, rather than focusing on the pursuit of new activities, MMF wished to consolidate the work of the past thirty years. The association determined that this objective required the complete renewal of the executive council's leadership with individuals who demonstrated a clear commitment to the church but who had not been previously involved in the association's activities. In a meeting of the general assembly in February 1984, members selected Marcel Masi as their new president and, two months later, designated Gilbert Klopfenstein as MMF's first French executive secretary.[6] These individuals set about implementing a mandate to strengthen the association's existing projects. MBM was supportive of MMF's new direction. However, the board did not wish to give up the possibility of opening new projects in the country. If MMF was unable to support new missionary ventures, MBM would now be able to explore opportunities with other partners.

Precisely at this time, several promising possibilities for collaborative action with new French Mennonite groups were emerging. In 1980, the French- and

4 Minutes of the Executive Council of MMF, 7 September 1982. Box 4, Folder 22. Mennonite Board of Missions Overseas Ministry Division Data Files Part 6, 1980–1984. IV/18/013-06. Mennonite Church USA Archives. Goshen, IN.

5 Pierre Sommer, "À la Mission Mennonite Française," *Christ Seul*, January 1983, 39–40.

6 Marcel Masi, "Faisons le Point!" *Christ Seul*, July 1984, 14.

German-speaking Mennonite conferences merged in Association des Églises Évangéliques Mennonites de France (AEEMF; Association of Evangelical Mennonite Churches of France).[7] This step signified the growing desire of Mennonites in France to work together despite the linguistic and cultural barriers that had emerged within the community following its settlement in the eastern part of the country in the early eighteenth century.[8] It promised to alter the structure of the national Mennonite church, which in the past had not exercised meaningful supervision of individual Mennonite projects or associations.[9]

7 This organization had officially provided a legal framework for the activities of all Mennonites in France since 1925 but in practice functioned as two structurally distinct conferences until 1980. Harold S. Bender and Richard D. Thiessen, "Association des Églises Évangéliques Mennonites de France," *Global Anabaptist Mennonite Encyclopedia Online*, http://www.gameo.org/encyclopedia/contents/A7974.html.

8 Pierre Sommer and Nanne van der Zijpp, "French-Speaking Mennonites," *Global Anabaptist Mennonite Encyclopedia Online*, http://www.gameo.org/encyclopedia/contents/french_speaking_mennonites.

9 Michel Paret, "L'Action Sociale Mennonite en France au XX° Siècle: Approches Diachronique et Analytique" (PhD diss., École Pratique des Hautes Études, Sorbonne, Paris, 1997), 390.

"Family photo" of Foyer Grebel Christian Community (1983)

In January of the following year, *Christ Seul* published the reflections of Ernest Hege and Ernest Nussbaumer, directors of Villa des Sapins and Les Amis de l'Atelier, respectively, who outlined how the new conference structure might take shape. They envisioned the creation of a federal structure of commissions, responsible to AEEMF, and assigned with supervisory responsibilities over the national church's social projects, evangelistic witness, and finances. Under their proposal, a "Social Work Commission" would oversee the work of the MMF workshops in Châtenay-Malabry and Hautefeuille and the Mennonite children's homes in eastern France. Composed of representatives of individual congregations and the projects' staffs and executive councils, the commission would seek to safeguard the Christian character of Mennonite social institutions by promoting adherence to the projects' original statutes, encouraging hiring of Christian staff, and serving as a structural link between the projects and individual congregations. Furthermore, by stimulating collaboration between projects, the commission hoped to help each institution keep up with changes in the development of services for people with developmental disabilities and mental health problems. In a similar fashion, the Mission-Evangelism Commission would seek to coordinate the Mennonite church's evangelistic activities. It would provide a forum for ongoing contact between the French Mennonite Mission Committee, MMF, and several smaller mission associations, through which its members would attempt to stimulate interest in missions by organizing meetings

and conferences, evaluating missionary methods, exploring collaboration with other evangelical groups and encouraging the founding of new Mennonite congregations.[10]

Both partners were excited about these developments. MBM staff recognized the potential for "better coordination of mission and service projects," while MMF saw an opportunity to integrate its evangelism and Christian service efforts into the larger work of AEEMF.[11] The association had always seen itself as "one of the instruments of French Mennonites for bringing the Good News to the French population in the name of Christ," and now it could pursue this calling as a recognized representative of the united national church.[12] Yet, as Pierre Sommer noted in *Christ*

---

10 Ernest Hege and Ernest Nussbaumer, "Reflexions sur le Role, la Composition et les Fonctions des Commissions," *Christ Seul*, January 1981, 20.

11 Robert Witmer, Report to MBM, 1980. Box 10, Folder 33. Mennonite Board of Missions Overseas Ministry Division Data Files Part 6, 1980–1984. IV/18/013-06. Mennonite Church USA Archives. Goshen, IN.

12 Robert Witmer, "Commencement d'une Ébauche de Texte . . .," 9 November 1982. Box 4, Folder 19. Mennonite Board of Missions Overseas Ministry Division Data Files Part 6,

Seul, it was not clear how MMF would fit into the new conference structure, given the range of its activities.[13] The implications of conference reorganization for the activity of MBM personnel in France were also unclear.[14] To whom would the North American missionaries be accountable? Might the Mission-Evangelism Commission be a more appropriate supervisory organization than MMF for MBM's missionary activity in France?[15] The uncertainty resulting from French Mennonite unification further influenced the redefinition of the MMF and MBM partnership relationship.

In September 1986, MBM administrator Wilbert Shenk met with Marcel Masi and Gilbert Klopfenstein for the first time following the establishment of this new framework. In this meeting, the representatives of MMF, which had recently demonstrated a desire to associate themselves with AEEMF,[16] confirmed that their primary objective remained the creation of churches in the greater Paris area. They no longer planned to pursue this goal with the interconfessional group at Verrières, whose trust had been lost with the Witmers' departure. Instead, Masi and Klopfenstein hoped that the MMF projects in the Paris region could serve as a fertile base for future evangelistic witness.[17] Nevertheless, although "numerous and exciting" possibilities for church-planting initiatives remained under discussion in the following years, they did not find concrete expression.[18] MMF was more comfortable with financing

1980–1984. IV/18/013-06. Mennonite Church USA Archives. Goshen, IN.

13 Pierre Sommer, "À la Mission Mennonite Française," *Christ Seul*, January 1983, 39–40.

14 Larry Miller, Annual Report for MBM France, 21 October 1980. Box 4. Mennonite Board of Missions Overseas Ministry Division Data Files Part 6, 1980–1984. IV/18/013-06. Mennonite Church USA Archives. Goshen, IN.

15 Robert Witmer to Wilbert Shenk, 25 October 1984. Box 4, Folder 19. Mennonite Board of Missions Overseas Ministry Division Data Files Part 6, 1980–1984. IV/18/013-06. Mennonite Church USA Archives. Goshen, IN.

16 Gilbert Klopfenstein, "Que Devient la Mission Mennonite Française?" *Christ Seul*, October 1986, 19.

17 Wilbert Shenk, Record of meeting with Marcel Masi and Gilbert Klopfenstein, 24 October 1986. Box 2, Folder 28. Mennonite Board of Missions Overseas Ministry Division Data Files Part 7, 1985–1990. IV/18/013-07. Mennonite Church USA Archives. Goshen, IN.

18 Neal Blough, "France," in MBM Annual Report, 1986, 105–7. Box 5, Folder 7. Mennonite Board of Missions Annual

evangelistic efforts than with engaging in these activities with its own personnel.

Diversification in the Partners' Work at Foyer Grebel, 1984-91

Now that Foyer Fraternel, Les Amis de l'Atelier, and Domaine Emmanuel operated exclusively under French Mennonite administration and supervision, Foyer Grebel became MMF and MBM's primary locus of collaboration. Like its supervisory association, the ministry to foreign students in Paris was undergoing significant changes. In July 1984, the Foyer Grebel executive council had drafted a new "Vision for the Future" to direct the ministry's future development.[19] The center's leadership proposed the purchase of a second facility, into which they would move the student residence. This would allow Foyer Grebel to double its lodging capacity, thereby providing relief from incessant rent increases for foreign students. At the same

Foyer Grebel Christian Community worship (early 1980s). Left to right: Senga Leao, Musese Luambo, Jibbée Njétein, and Danhré Lambert (later director of Foyer Grebel Maisons-Alfort)

time, this expansion would free space at the existing location for the creation of a center for reflection and study, to be directed and staffed by Neal and Janie Blough. Furthermore, the council's members believed that the separation of the student ministry from the Communauté Chrétienne du Foyer Grebel would

---

Meeting Minutes and Annual Reports, 1900–2000. IV/06/003. Mennonite Church USA Archives, Goshen, IN.

19 Proposal to be submitted to the 28 February 1986 Meeting of the Executive Council of Foyer Grebel, undated, Foyer Grebel Archive, Centre Mennonite de Paris, France.

affirm the congregation's identity as an independent body and encourage the community to turn its attention to local outreach.[20] Both branches of Foyer Grebel would remain connected in name, administration, and programming. The executive council would be charged with "watching that the social project not become more important than the spiritual project, particularly in the level of interest brought by each partner to the different areas of work."[21]

Centre 21

In January 1986, the Foyer Grebel executive council presented MMF with a proposal to purchase three homes at 21, rue Bourgelat in the nearby suburb of Maisons-Alfort, two for student residences and one for the director couple, Denis and Lydia Schultz. The association considered the proposed expansion feasible, given that it benefited from multiple sources of funding and would

20 Neal Blough and Denis Schultz, "Projet d'Extension à Maisons-Alfort, Objectifs de l'Opération," 22 January 1986, Foyer Grebel Archive, Centre Mennonite de Paris, France; Neal Blough, "France," in MBM Annual Report, 1986, 105–7. Box 5, Folder 7. Mennonite Board of Missions Annual Meeting Minutes and Annual Reports, 1900–2000. IV/06/003. Mennonite Church USA Archives, Goshen, IN.

21 Minutes of the Executive Council of Foyer Grebel, 5 July 1986, Foyer Grebel Archive, Centre Mennonite de Paris, France.

Early work on Maisons-Alfort facility

require no new staff.[22] A state-run immigrant housing fund would provide a low-interest loan to cover renovation expenses and half the purchase cost, and MMF, MBM, and Europäisches Mennonitisches Evangelisationskomitee (EMEK; European Mennonite Missions Committee) would lend Foyer Grebel the balance of the required money, which would be repaid through residents' monthly rental dues.[23]

MMF purchased the property in July and the Schultzes prepared it to receive its first residents by December of the following year.[24] A ceremony of inauguration of Centre 21, as the new facility was informally named, was held in March 1988.[25] Marcel Masi presided over the service of dedication, which was attended by the city's mayor and representatives of MMF,

Hotsche Kikkert with Jean-Luc Husser, a French Mennonite conscientious objector, at Maisons-Alfort facility (ca. 1985)

22 Minutes of the Executive Council of MMF, 4 January 1986, personal files of Robert Witmer, Cambridge, ON.

23 Ibid.

24 Denis Schultz, Activity Report, October 1987–January 1988, Foyer Grebel Archive, Centre Mennonite de Paris, France.

25 Foyer Grebel's two new centers were informally named Centre 21 and Centre 13, after their respective addresses: 21, rue Bourgelat, Maisons-Alfort, and 13, Val d'Osne, Saint Maurice.

EMEK, Association des Églises Évangéliques Mennonites de France, and the French Mennonite Missions
Committee.[26] The residence soon reached its capacity
of twenty-four students, continuing in its mission to
provide them with a temporary home as they settled
into a new and often inhospitable environment. "Even
if we constitute only the smallest contribution in an
ocean of needs," Denis Schultz wrote in *Christ Seul*,
"we hope that this contribution might be added to the
Lord's edifice."[27]

Following the new center's opening, a small committee, composed of Christian residents and members
of Communauté Chrétienne du Foyer Grebel (CCFG),
planned regular activities that encouraged the creation
of a close-knit student community.[28] In an effort to
maintain Centre 21's Christian character, the center's
personnel organized weekly Bible studies for residents
and staff from Centre 13, as the original Foyer Grebel

location was now informally named. These meetings
promoted maintenance of close ties between the two
projects which, while pursuing related goals, were to
differ substantially in their approaches.

Centre 13/Centre Mennonite d'Études et de Rencontres (CMER)

At Centre 13, the Foyer Grebel executive council envisioned development of a missionary project that differed markedly from the type of work in which MMF
and MBM had previously engaged. They wished to create a Mennonite center, based on the model of those
in London and Brussels, which would foster study and
promotion of Anabaptist theology.[29] Initially, Centre
Mennonite d'Études et de Rencontres (Mennonite
Study and Meeting Center) would consist of a library,
reading room, and space to host short-term visitors.[30]
Janie and Neal Blough would assume responsibility for
directing, staffing, and administering the center.

In many ways, this project reflected the thirty-year-
old vision of David Shank, former MBM missionary

---

26 Denis Schultz, "L'Inauguration du Nouveau Centre 21,"
Christ Seul, May 1988, 14–15.

27 Ibid.

28 Minutes of the Executive Council of Foyer Grebel, 23
January 1988; and Denis Schultz, Activity Report, October
1987–January 1988, Foyer Grebel Archive, Centre Mennonite
de Paris, France.

29 Neal Blough, interview by David Neufeld, 7 June 2012.

30 Proposal to be submitted to the 28 February 1986 Meeting of the Executive Council of Foyer Grebel, undated, Foyer
Grebel Archive, Centre Mennonite de Paris, France.

Some of the Foyer Grebel staff (early 1980s). Left to right: Denis Schultz, Hotsche Kikkert, Neal Blough, André Hege, Martica Hege, and Lydia Schultz

to Belgium, who had argued that missions in "dechristianized" urban environments could most effectively be carried out through a "live spiritual center," dedicated to historical, theological, and cultural study and animated by "Spirit-led, almost charismatic" corporate worship.[31] For the CMER leadership, Shank's model remained compelling because of the ongoing relevance of the missiological challenges to which it responded.

How can Christians live in the world without being of the world? In a seemingly hopeless and violent environment, how can they best offer God's word of hope, love, reconciliation, and justice? How should Anabaptist Mennonites express their specificity in a context that is suspicious of Christian truth claims?[32] Although MMF and MBM personnel had been wrestling with these questions for decades, CMER organizers hoped to create a forum in which they could be addressed more intentionally, in discussion with other Christian groups. They hoped to convene interconfessional conferences and to allot greater resources and staff time to teaching in evangelical and Protestant educational institutions.[33] Vitally, the center's witness would be reinforced by the ongoing presence of Communauté Chrétienne du Foyer Grebel in the building, which would provide "a framework in which we can live the Gospel that we wish to faithfully proclaim."[34]

---

31 Shank, "A Missionary Approach," 53–54.

32 Neal Blough, "Centre Mennonite d'Études et de Rencontres Saint-Maurice," *Christ Seul*, January 1995, 14–15.

33 Proposal to be submitted to the 28 February 1986 Meeting of the Executive Council of Foyer Grebel, undated, Foyer Grebel Archive, Centre Mennonite de Paris, France.

34 Ibid.

Foyer Grebel Christmas celebration, early 1980s

CMER activities enjoyed early success. The first seminars were well attended. AEEMF and local Mennonite congregations invited CMER staff and associates to coordinate study and reflection on pressing issues such as the remuneration of pastors and the proper relationship between congregations and Mennonite social work institutions.[35] French conscientious objectors and a North American volunteer collected, classified, and computerized a growing collection of books and periodicals dealing with Anabaptist and Mennonite history and theology, missions, and peace and justice issues.[36] Soon the library had a network of paying members who benefited from the harmonization of

35 Josette Peterschmitt, Minutes of the Executive Council of Foyer Grebel, 6 January 1990, Foyer Grebel Archive, Centre Mennonite de Paris, France; "France," in MBM Annual Report, 1991, OV 20–22. Box 6, Folder 4. Mennonite Board of Missions Annual Meeting Minutes and Annual Reports, 1900–2000. IV/06/003. Mennonite Church USA Archives, Goshen, IN.

36 "France," in MBM Annual Report, 1990, OV 24. Box 6, Folder 3. Mennonite Board of Missions Annual Meeting Minutes and Annual Reports, 1900–2000. IV/06/003. Mennonite Church USA Archives, Goshen, IN; Neal and Janie Blough, CMER Report prepared for the Executive Council of Foyer Grebel, June 1991; and minutes of the Executive Council of

the classification systems of the libraries of CMER, the Bible Institute of Nogent-sur-Marne, and the Evangelical Faculty at Vaux-sur-Seine.[37] Blough taught several courses at Vaux but dedicated the majority of his efforts to the strengthening of the study center for students interested in Anabaptism.[38] In 1988, MBM's teaching capacities in France increased when Linda Oyer began her missionary service as academic dean and dean of faculty at the evangelical European Bible Institute at Lamorlaye. In addition to providing a Mennonite presence and witness in this international and interdenominational school, she taught periodically for the Bienenberg, a bilingual Mennonite Bible school located near Basel, Switzerland.[39]

In 1988, Linda Oyer joined the Mennonite Board of Missions team. She has taught in a variety of church-affiliated educational institutions in France and Switzerland.

Functioning alongside CMER, CCFG also experienced positive growth. Although the transitory nature of its membership had created instability in the past, the congregation of nearly seventy participants now benefited from a stable core, which included members

Foyer Grebel, 12 October 1991, Foyer Grebel Archive, Centre Mennonite de Paris, France.

37 E. Kennel, Minutes of the Executive Council of Foyer Grebel, 4 February 1989; and minutes of the Executive Council of Foyer Grebel, 5 January 1991, Foyer Grebel Archive, Centre Mennonite de Paris, France.

38 Minutes of the Management Council of Foyer Grebel, 4 October 1994, Foyer Grebel Archive, Centre Mennonite de Paris, France.

39 "France," in MBM Annual Report, 1990, OV 23–25. Box 6, Folder 3. Mennonite Board of Missions Annual Meeting

Minutes and Annual Reports, 1900–2000. IV/06/003. Mennonite Church USA Archives, Goshen, IN.

Prayer during the ordination service of Patrick Monard (kneeling) at Foyer Grebel Christian Community. Left to right (standing): Danrhé Lambert, Richard Vandebroucque, Neal Blough, Damaris Hege, and Djamba Djulu.

who had joined from Foyer Fraternel in Châtenay-Malabry to support CCFG.[40] With worshipers from Zaire, Cameroon, Angola, North America, and France, including residents from Centre 21, the congregation drew strength and inspiration from its cultural and racial diversity.[41] Neal Blough's leadership responsibilities, which included coordinating and planning worship, preaching, leading weekly Bible studies, visiting members, and meeting with other church leaders, were slowly being passed off to other members. In 1990, CCFG initiated a two-year congregational discernment process that concluded with the selection of a pastoral team and group of elders and the implementation of a new structure for congregational decision making.[42] Together, the community sought to confront the chal-

---

40 Larry Miller, Annual Report for MBM France, 1986. Box 2, Folder 28. Mennonite Board of Missions Overseas Ministry Division Data Files Part 7, 1985–1990. IV/18/013-07.

Mennonite Church USA Archives. Goshen, IN; and Neal Blough, "France," in MBM Annual Report, 1986, 105–7. Box 5, Folder 7. Mennonite Board of Missions Annual Meeting Minutes and Annual Reports, 1900–2000. IV/06/003. Mennonite Church USA Archives, Goshen, IN.

41 Neal Blough, "Croissance là où tout est neuf," *Christ Seul*, January 1989, 12–13.

42 "France," in MBM Annual Report, 1990, OV 25. Box 6, Folder 3. Mennonite Board of Missions Annual Meeting Minutes and Annual Reports, 1900–2000. IV/06/003. Mennonite Church USA Archives, Goshen, IN; and "Communauté Chrétienne du Foyer Grebel," *Christ Seul*, January 1992, 16–17.

lenge of "how to announce and live the Gospel in a seemingly indifferent urban environment."[43]

The simultaneous growth of CCFG and CMER resulted in an increased demand for shared space. Cognizant of the difficulties and conflicts that the complex of church and workshop had created at Châtenay-Malabry, Janie and Neal Blough expressed their desire that CMER and CCFG be given room to develop independently, while retaining ties to each other.[44] In light of this concern, MBM representatives recommended initiation of a search for a new building for the congregation. The Foyer Grebel executive council shared this determination, and presented the plan to the congregation in October 1991.[45] CCFG accepted the proposal and began to look for a new home. To aid in this pursuit,

MMF offered the congregation an interest-free loan for 60 percent of the new building's cost. MBM promised

Foyer Grebel women. Left to right: Marie-Claire Fatuma, Martine Ehrismann Solomiac, Lydia Schultz, Juliette Ndilkei, Françoise Awezaï, Janie Blough, and Doris Schrock (North American Mennonite volunteer).

43 Neal Blough, "Croissance là où tout est neuf," *Christ Seul,* January 1989, 12–13.

44 Neal and Janie Blough, Mennonite Board of Missions Quarterly Report, February-April 1991. Box 1, Folder 73. Mennonite Board of Missions Overseas Ministry Division Data Files Part 8, 1990–1995. IV/18/013-08. Mennonite Church USA Archives. Goshen, IN.

45 Minutes of the Executive Council of Foyer Grebel, 12 October 1991, Foyer Grebel Archive, Centre Mennonite de Paris, France.

to donate $100,000 to capital expenses, to be paid over five years.[46]

MMF Raises Questions about Its Structure, 1992-93

The provision of funds to evangelistic efforts such as CCFG continued to form an important part of MMF activity. During the 1990s, the association made loans available to the biblical and theological training centers at Nogent-sur-Marne and Vaux-sur-Seine.[47] It subsidized operating costs of Action Sociale et Évangile by paying for secretarial help, and it helped finance Joie et Vie (Joy and Life) and Laisse-moi Te Raconter . . . (Let Me Tell You . . .), a Christian summer camp and children's choir, respectively.[48] MMF contributed to the travel costs of a CCFG choir tour to the United States[49] and donated money to AEEMF to help an Af-

rican delegate attend Mennonite World Conference in Calcutta.[50] Yet MMF's ability to respond favorably to frequent requests for financial support from a wide variety of mission and service organizations diminished over time.

Telling the Foyer Grebel story at a variety of French Mennonite and other evangelical gatherings. Left to right: Janie Blough with Elisabeth and Charles Khrossad at European Mennonite Conference (Colmar 1993)

---

46 Ibid.

47 Minutes of the Executive Council of MMF, 9 September 1993 and 20 December 1993, AEDE Archive, Hautefeuille, France.

48 Minutes of the Executive Council of MMF, 21 April 1995, AEDE Archive, Hautefeuille, France.

49 Ibid.

---

50 Minutes of the Executive Council of MMF, 1 December 1995, AEDE Archive, Hautefeuille, France.

The association's financial flexibility had long been dependent on French Mennonite loans and donations to the association through Service Épargne Mennonite (SEM; Mennonite Savings Service). Over time, these contributions decreased notably, in large part because of the widely held but mistaken assumption that the state provided MMF with funding to support each of its mission and service activities.[51] In reality, the French government strictly regulated the use of excess income generated by the association's state-funded institution, Domaine Emmanuel.[52] State subsidies for the operation of the Centre d'aide par le travail at Hautefeuille, even if they exceeded the center's needs, could not be redirected toward evangelistic projects. The association was reluctant to liquidate its property holdings to fund these efforts.

In the face of these financial realities, MMF increasingly directed its effort and attention to the financially sustainable area of its activity: its medical and educational services to youth with developmental disabilities at Hautefeuille.[53] This gradual but noticeable shift in the association's priorities did not occasion an immediate disassociation from the comprehensive missionary model that combined evangelism and service. The MMF statutes still placed efforts "to make known the Word of God and the Gospel of our Savior Jesus Christ to men of our time who do not have the pleasure of knowing them" at the heart of the association's mission.[54] In pursuit of this end, MMF representatives took an active role in supporting formation of the Missionary Department of AEEMF, which embodied a renewed attempt by the national church to coordinate the French Mennonite missionary witness both inside and outside the country.[55] Nevertheless, while MMF remained sensitive to questions about the evangelistic character of its institutions and expressed interest in creating stronger ties to the French Mennonite church,

---

51 Théo Hege, e-mail message to author, 15 June 2012.

52 Victor Hugo Dos Santos, "Mission Mennonite Française," *Christ Seul*, January 1998, 36–38.

53 Gilbert Klopfenstein, "Mission Mennonite Française," *Christ Seul*, January 1989, 28.

54 Annual Report of the MMF General Assembly, 1993, Foyer Grebel Archive, Centre Mennonite de Paris, France.

55 Minutes of the Executive Council of MMF, 2 December 1994, 8 October 1995, and 7 February 1996, AEDE Archive, Hautefeuille, France.

it took steps to clarify whether its existing structure, statutes, and name fit its emerging identity.

In November 1992, at the request of new president Joël Haldemann, MMF convened a commission to discuss its future. At a retreat attended by Neal Blough, MMF executive secretary Gilbert Klopfenstein, Foyer Grebel executive council president René Peterschmitt, Domaine Emmanuel director Victor Dos Santos, and Centre 21 director Aboh Lambert Danrhé (who, with his wife, Louise, had replaced Denis and Lydia Schultz in 1990), delegates discussed possibilities for reorganization of MMF administration and operation. Among a variety of other options, they considered establishment of complete legal and administrative autonomy for MMF, Foyer Grebel, and Domaine Emmanuel. This alternative was discarded in favor of a restructuring of the existing model. In the future, Domaine Emmanuel and Foyer Grebel would be administered by separate management councils. These bodies would hold greater decision-making power and autonomy vis-à-vis MMF, whose executive council would meet primarily to assure the legal functioning of the two ministries.[56] This

Lambert and Louise Danrhé, who replaced Denis and Lydia Schultz as director-couple of the Foyer Grebel Maison-Alfort

56 Report of the "Avenir MMF" commission, 13 November 1992, Foyer Grebel Archive, Centre Mennonite de Paris, France.

new arrangement provided a structural guarantee of ongoing communication within the association and ensured that each of the MMF projects enjoyed structural equality.[57] It also transferred the onus for determining the vision of Foyer Grebel from MMF to the center itself.

While the MMF reorganization purposefully sought to keep the association's partnership with MBM intact, it engendered a change in the conditions of the partnership in a number of ways. First, the decision removed MBM representation from the MMF executive council. The North American agency's primary channel of communication with its French partner shifted to the Foyer Grebel management council. In this body, the board's interests were communicated by staff members Neal and Janie Blough, whom the council supervised, and MBM representatives Linda Oyer and Robert Charles, the latter now supervising MBM activity in France after the brief terms of service of Larry Miller and Alice Roth. At a more basic level, the commission's decision meant that MMF itself no longer held the same responsibility for the spiritual supervision of MBM personnel in France or their activities at Centre Mennonite d'Études et de Rencontres (CMER). The North American board, through its workers in France, progressively took up this task in conjunction with existing partners and individuals and groups that became associated with CMER over the coming years.

These deliberations represented the first official exchange in a decade-long discussion within the association about the character of its identity. Did the association wish to remain an evangelistic organization, or would it focus exclusively on providing social services to less privileged members of society? Could it continue to hold these two objectives together as part of a broader mission strategy, as the French association and MBM had done together in the past? The altered statutes adopted by the MMF 1993 general assembly in light of the commission's decision indicated that it hoped to try. The association now intended "to create . . . manage, run and inspect health, socio-medical, socio-educative, and lodging facilities," but also left its other statutes, which had guided the association's activity since 1965, in place.[58] Yet, the course of the association's deliberations over the next years led consistently

57 Ibid.

58 Annual Report of the MMF General Assembly, 1993, Foyer Grebel Archive, Centre Mennonite de Paris, France.

in the direction of a separation between the two avenues of its activity.

Developments in the Partners' Projects Encourage a Reevaluation of Their Relationship, 1991–2001

The Closing of Centre 21 and Foyer Bethanie, EMEK Withdraws Support for Foyer Grebel

Over the next years, there was diminishing overlap in the areas of activity of MMF and MBM. Developments in each of the MMF projects over this period encouraged this tendency. The breakdown of the model of united evangelistic and social activity at Foyer Grebel, occasioned by the closing of Centre 21, was particularly significant. In June 1991, just one year after Aboh Lambert Danrhé had been appointed by the Foyer Grebel executive council as director of the student residence, he had received notice from the municipality of Maisons-Alfort that Centre 21, along with 60 percent of the buildings in its neighborhood, had been declared a Zone d'aménagement concertée (ZAC; Zone of Planned Development), as part of a government rezoning initiative which attempted to promote urban development.[59] A local official had informed him that welcoming foreign students to France did not represent a service to the country, and that the Foyer Grebel residence would be demolished and replaced by offices, educational facilities, retirement homes, and low-income housing.[60] Convinced that the decision to demolish Centre 21 had not been made fairly, Danhré led an effort of the Foyer Grebel leadership to challenge the municipality's plans, most noticeably through participation in Rénov'Alfort, a neighborhood association that initially succeeded in delaying the development project.[61]

With the threat of demolition hanging over Centre 21, several other developments brought the student ministry's future into question. In 1993, the French,

---

59 Minutes of the Executive Council of Foyer Grebel, 29 June 1991, Foyer Grebel Archive, Centre Mennonite de Paris, France; and Aboh Lambert Danrhé, "Foyer Grebel," *Christ Seul*, January 1992, 7–8.

60 Aboh Lambert Danrhé to Prefect of Maisons-Alfort, 2 November 1992, Foyer Grebel Archive, Centre Mennonite de Paris, France.

61 Aboh Lambert Danrhé, "Foyer Grebel," *Christ Seul*, January 1993, 11–12; and Aboh Lambert Danrhé, "Foyer Grebel," *Christ Seul*, January 1994, 22–23.

Dutch, Swiss, and German mission committees ended their forty-three-year collaboration in EMEK.[62] As a result, the European committee's funding to Foyer Grebel was cut.[63] The center still benefited from the support of the French Mennonite Mission Committee and later developed a relationship with the Dutch Mennonite Mission (DZR), primarily through Foyer Grebel executive committee member Jakob Kikkert. Nevertheless, Foyer Grebel had lost an important partner and source of financial support. The closing of Foyer Bethanie in January 1995 caused the center further disappointment. The Baptist Church of the Tabernacle repossessed the building, forcing staff to begin the difficult task of finding alternative housing for the center's residents.[64] The loss of Bethanie seriously weakened the student center's lodging network.

Soon afterward, the department of Val de Marne accepted Maisons-Alfort's second urban development proposal, an action that guaranteed Centre 21's eventual demolition.[65] In light of this decision, the Foyer Grebel management council reached out to its partners in order to clarify their objectives and interests regarding the continuation of its ministry to African students. The French Mennonite Mission Committee, desiring to rededicate itself exclusively to foreign missions, indicated that it would end its relationship with Foyer Grebel.[66] While pledging its ongoing support for work with foreign students and expressing appreciation for its partnership with the French and Dutch mission committees and MBM, MMF reminded the Foyer Grebel management council that it had been delegated full responsibility for clarifying its own vision and goals.[67] MMF no longer considered this task as its responsibility.

As a consequence, the Foyer Grebel leadership began a process of reflection about their motivations and

62 Pierre Lugbull, "La Mission Mennonite à un tournant," *Christ Seul*, February 1994, 11–12.

63 Aboh Lambert Danrhé, "Foyer Grebel," *Christ Seul*, January 1993, 11–12.

64 Minutes of the Management Council of Foyer Grebel, 4 October 1994, Foyer Grebel Archive, Centre Mennonite de Paris, France.

65 Minutes of the Executive Council of MMF, 21 April 1995, AEDE Archive, Hautefeuille, France.

66 Minutes of the Executive Council of MMF, 6 December 1996, AEDE Archive, Hautefeuille, France.

67 Minutes of the Executive Council of Foyer Grebel, 20 April 1996, Foyer Grebel Archive, Centre Mennonite de Paris, France.

The Foyer Fraternel congregation in Châtenay-Malabry, south of Paris, in 2013

vision for future work, and the needs to which they wished to respond. With MMF help, they explored the possibility of converting the Foyer Grebel student residence into a Centre d'Hébergement et de Réinsertion Sociale (Housing and Social Rehabilitation Center), which would be eligible for state subsidies.[68] The committee's belief that it would be impossible to maintain the missionary quality of the center if they accepted state funding led them to discard this option.[69] While the council remained convinced that "the Church has a role to play in relating to foreigners in our country," it concluded that "at the current time no project has been proposed and it is unlikely that any work can be initiated by the time of the residence's closing."[70] Foyer Grebel's Centre 21 shut down in June 1998. MMF negotiated compensation for the property, and designated

a part of the funds to subsidize the residents' and staff's search for lodging.[71]

The Growth and Development of Domaine Emmanuel and Centre Mennonite d'Études et de Rencontres

The closing of the Foyer Grebel student ministry coincided paradoxically with the thirty-year anniversary of Domaine Emmanuel. The success of the Centre d'aide par le travail at Hautefeuille, which now served both young men and women, was a product of the quality of its medical and educational services and its ability to adapt to the changing standards of the state and the companies that contracted work out to its residents. The facility had developed into "an establishment open to the outside world, well integrated into the village and credible vis-à-vis supervisory authorities."[72] The positive reputation earned by MMF facilitated further growth, which began with the founding of the Résidence Simeon in Coulommiers in 1997, a center that welcomed adults over the age of forty-five with developmental disabilities and mental health conditions.

---

68 Minutes of the Executive Council of MMF, 26 May 1997, AEDE Archive, Hautefeuille, France.

69 E. Zemlanski-Weber, Minutes of Foyer Grebel Management Council, 4 October 1997, Foyer Grebel Archive, Centre Mennonite de Paris, France.

70 Ibid.

71 Minutes of the Executive Council of MMF, 12 May 1998, AEDE Archive, Hautefeuille, France.

72 Christine de Coninck and Annick Dubois, "La Fête à Hautefeuille," *Christ Seul*, November 1993, 24–25.

Since the 1970s, the French association had explored the possibility of establishing a home for older graduates of its Centre d'aide par le travail.[73] In the intervening period, the life expectancy of individuals in France with developmental disabilities and mental health conditions had increased dramatically, in part as a result of the innovative services provided by facilities such as Domaine Emmanuel. This trend made the newest MMF project viable and necessary in the eyes of the state. Résidence Simeon became one of the first institutions of its kind in France.[74] In the next three years, MMF established a similar home in Nanteuil-les-Meaux and founded a center that specialized in providing psychiatric care. For the association's leadership, these facilities formed part of a growing network of services for adults with developmental disabilities and mental health conditions, which complemented the care provided by the Centre d'aide par le travail in Hautefeuille.[75]

The efforts of CMER associates and staff, which Linda Oyer joined after the European Bible Institute closed in 1998, also continued to bear fruit. Although not directly related to the activity of the center, the emergence in 1997 of a third Mennonite congregation in the region had resulted from Oyer's participation with other Mennonites in a group of theological reflection and fellowship in the suburb of Lamorlaye. As part of a team of five, Oyer now helped lead the new church of thirty members.[76] At the same time, she strengthened the teaching outreach capacity of CMER, which contributed to the center's long-standing goal of "presenting and strengthening an Anabaptist perspective in a context where Christianity had become marginal, and is seen to be irrelevant to the larger society."[77]

73 Minutes of the MMF General Assembly, 30 September 1973, photocopy of *Cahier Officiel* of MMF, personal files of Robert Witmer, Cambridge, ON.

74 Mathieu Oui, "Une maison de retraite pour handicapés s'ouvre dans les Hauts-de-Seine," *La Croix*, 24 May 1996.

75 Minutes of the Executive Council of MMF, 16 November 2001, AEDE Archive, Hautefeuille, France.

76 "France," in MBM Annual Report, 1995, 25–26. Box 6, Folder 6. Mennonite Board of Missions Annual Meeting Minutes and Annual Reports, 1900–2000. IV/06/003. Mennonite Church USA Archives, Goshen, IN.; and "France," in MBM Annual Report, 1997, 39–40. Box 6, Folder 7. Mennonite Board of Missions Annual Meeting Minutes and Annual Reports, 1900–2000. IV/06/003. Mennonite Church USA Archives, Goshen, IN.

77 "France," in MBM Annual Report, 1994, 40–41. Box 6, Folder 5. Mennonite Board of Missions Annual Meeting

During this period, CMER significantly expanded its field of action, seeking to extend its promotion of Anabaptist Mennonite theology into the broader French-speaking world.[78] In France, this objective took many forms. The center continued to sponsor interconfessional study groups, colloquiums, and seminars in an effort to contribute to ecumenical theological and missiological discussions. The center's library received a small but steady stream of French and foreign students from evangelical, Protestant, Catholic, and secular institutions interested in Anabaptist Mennonite theology and history. Most significantly, CMER helped create an academic training program administered by a network of francophone educational institutions. Beginning in 1998, Neal Blough and Claude Baecher of Centre de Formation et de Rencontre Bienenberg (CEFOR; Bienenberg Training and Meeting Center) began conversations that resulted in the creation of the Études Francophones en Théologie Anabaptiste (EFraTA;

Francophone Studies in Anabaptist Theology) program, which came to offer seminary level courses in Anabaptist history and theology to those interested in pastoral or diaconal service.[79] The academic partnership of CMER and CEFOR was further bolstered by their collaborative development of a publication series tackling historical, ethical, ecclesiological, and theological questions. In November 2001, the French evangelical publishing house Excelsis released the first volume in the Perspectives Anabaptistes series.[80]

CMER also became involved in an international francophone network, following the 1997 visit of Neal Blough and Juan José Romero, director of Brussels Mennonite Center, to Kinshasa, Democratic Republic of Congo. In conversation with Congolese Anabaptists, the visitors learned that Mennonites there wished to create an official relationship with European Mennonite churches. On their return, Blough and Romero

Minutes and Annual Reports, 1900–2000. IV/06/003. Mennonite Church USA Archives, Goshen, IN.

78 "France," in MBM Annual Report, 1999, 44–45. Box 8, Folder 7. Mennonite Board of Missions Annual Meeting Minutes and Annual Reports, 1900–2000. IV/06/003. Mennonite Church USA Archives, Goshen, IN.

79 Ibid.; Minutes of the Management Council of CMER, 14 May 2001, Foyer Grebel Archive, Centre Mennonite de Paris, France.

80 Minutes of the Management Council of CMER, 15 May 2000, Foyer Grebel Archive, Centre Mennonite de Paris, France; "Assemblée Générale 2002, Mission Mennonite Française," 19.

reported this news to Mennonite World Conference, which organized a delegation of eight French, Swiss, Belgian, Dutch, and Canadian Mennonites that returned to Congo in 1999. These representatives established official links with the leadership of the Anabaptist churches in the country.[81] After this point, the interested parties turned to MWC for guidance and oversight, and an international francophone network was eventually structured under this organization's auspices. In Europe, following the visit of a return delegation of Congolese and Québécois in 2001, the newly formed Franco-Swiss Comité Européen du Réseau Francophone (European Committee of the Francophone Network) began to convene biannual meetings for representatives of European Mennonite conferences and organizations wishing to participate in the network. CMER's continuous support for the network helped make the center more visible in the francophone Mennonite world.

The expansion of the vision and activity of CMER placed growing pressure on the limited space in the MMF house in Saint Maurice, which the center continued to share with the Blough family and Communauté Chrétienne du Foyer Grebel (CCFG). These circumstances lent greater urgency to the CMER directors' calls for the congregation to find a new church home. In 1996, representatives of the Foyer Grebel management council, MMF, and MBM had reiterated their desire that the facility in Saint Maurice be used exclusively for the operation of CMER.[82] Yet, the congregation's repeated efforts to purchase an alternative meeting place had been unsuccessful. In various instances, municipal officials, property owners, and neighborhood associations had blocked church representatives' attempts. "Is it truly impossible to establish a new Church building in an urban center today?" member Frédéric de Coninck wondered.[83] As a result of these failures, the CCFG leadership advocated ongoing joint use of the building and altered the congregation's programming to accommodate the activities of CMER and

---

81 Minutes of the Executive Council of MMF, 7 December 1998, AEDE Archive, Hautefeuille, France; Neal Blough, interview by David Neufeld, 7 June 2012.

82 Minutes of the Executive Council of MMF, 6 December 1996, AEDE Archive, Hautefeuille, France.

83 Frédéric de Coninck, "Saint-Maurice," *Christ Seul*, January 1999, 7.

the Bloughs.[84] They were frustrated by the decision of the CMER management council, supported by both MMF and MBM, which did not change.[85] "The fact that CMER and CCFG have more or less evolved together in the same place with the presence of the same people involved in the direction of both entities has led to institutional confusion and a lack of clarity with regard to the identity of each one," the center's board stated. "It is not positive to keep the center and church together. Both sets of activities are mutually disruptive."[86] The CCFG membership did not welcome this decision but continued their search for a new building.

The Separation of Social Work and Evangelistic Activities, 1996–2003

As a result of this series of developments in each of the MMF projects during this period, the association's leadership became increasingly convinced that the continued coexistence of evangelistic and social work within the same organization was no longer tenable. Financial constraints were a primary concern. Because of the disengagement of EMEK and the French Mennonite Mission Committee, CMER and Foyer Grebel—until its closure—ran annual deficits that MMF was not in a position to cover indefinitely.[87] In a May 1996 meeting of the MMF executive council, president Joël Haldeman had again drawn members' attention to the need for "a restructuring of the association taking into account in an effective manner the diversity of its bases of action."[88] He advocated for the complete administrative separation of the institutions providing social services—Domaine Emmanuel and the student

---

84 Claire-Lise Dos Santos to Joël Haldemann, 15 April 1998; and Claire-Lise Dos Santos to the CMER Management Council, 18 October 1999, Foyer Grebel Archive, Centre Mennonite de Paris, France.

85 E-mail message from Robert Charles to Neal Blough, 10 May 1998, Foyer Grebel Archive, Centre Mennonite de Paris, France; Minutes of the Executive Council of MMF, 23 May 2000, AEDE Archive, Hautefeuille, France.

86 Minutes of the CMER Management Council, 15 May 2000, Foyer Grebel Archive, Centre Mennonite de Paris, France.

---

87 Minutes of the MMF General Assembly, 14 June 1997, in the Annual Report of the MMF General Assembly, 1998, 25, personal files of Robert Witmer, Cambridge, ON.

88 Minutes of the Executive Council of MMF, 20 May 1996, AEDE Archive, Hautefeuille, France.

residence of Foyer Grebel—from those dedicated to evangelism—CMER and other associations supported by MMF funds. "The social action sector . . . would live in closer partnership with public authorities," he proposed. Meanwhile, "the evangelistic action sector . . . would be closer to local churches with which it would need to establish links of partnership."[89] The MMF leadership believed that this new arrangement would resolve its financial concerns and foster the creation of new partnerships that would prove more productive for all areas of its activity in the long term.

Haldemann's proposal, although it did not take immediate effect, promised to further diminish points of contact between MMF and MBM. Despite the implications of this recommendation for the organizations' partnership, MBM administration and personnel in France accepted its rationale over the next years. The board maintained an exclusive interest in projects with evangelistic goals. It now saw its mission in France as an effort to promote Anabaptist theology in conversation with Christians from other traditions; to participate in the creation of a network of francophone Anabaptists; and "to develop, together with the French Mennonite Conference, a relevant missiological approach in a highly urbanized and secularized context."[90] These objectives were being carried out most clearly in the work of CMER. It had become evident that the respective activities of CMER and MMF were of distinct natures, that the procedures by which they made decisions differed, and that they drew on distinct sources of support and finance. Both CMER and the other MMF projects had developed relationships with a variety of other entities. The benefits of mutual dependency no longer outweighed the drawbacks. Thus, when Haldemann proposed in a meeting of the center's management council in October 1999 that CMER become an autonomous association, representatives of other partner organizations responded favorably.[91] Each reaffirmed the importance of CMER for advancing Anabaptist Mennonite interests in Paris and in France, and each supported Neal and Janie Blough's continued involvement

89 Ibid.

90 "France," in MBM Annual Report, 1994, 40–41. Box 6, Folder 5. Mennonite Board of Missions Annual Meeting Minutes and Annual Reports, 1900–2000. IV/06/003. Mennonite Church USA Archives, Goshen, IN.

91 Minutes of the CMER Management Council, 26 October 1999, Foyer Grebel Archive, Centre Mennonite de Paris, France.

in the center.[92] Although the details of this process of separation took several years to work out, it was clear that MMF no longer wished to be involved in the administration or operation of the center.

The CMER leaders' willingness to work independently from MMF gave the association's executive council an opportunity to bring long deliberations about its institutional identity to a close. In a meeting of MMF general assembly in June 2001, the council presented members with an "MMF Development Proposal" prepared by Christine de Coninck. In it, the council observed that confusion and a lack of consensus about the organization's objectives remained. They wished to clarify the existing state of affairs. The four MMF facilities for people with developmental disabilities now served more than 200 individuals, employed more than 160 salaried staff, and had a combined budget of more than €10,000,000. Meanwhile, CMER represented less than one percent of the association's operational budget and had expressed a desire to work autonomously. As a result, the council proposed to "become what we are," an association dedicated solely to the provision of social or sociomedical services, "without giving up our values."[93] This course would require administrative restructuring and significant future expansion in order to optimize financial and management resources. In the interests of institutional clarity, and to prevent difficulties with state authorities who were unwilling to fund private religious associations, members were asked to consider adopting a new name for the association "appropriate to its purpose."[94]

In summary, the council continued, MMF faced a stark choice. Its members could decide to forego future growth in the interests of maintaining a "family atmosphere" or out of fear of putting the association's Christian identity at risk. Or the association could expand "to ensure consistent support and establish the association's longevity." The leadership believed that "the familial stage has already passed and has been replaced by greater professionalism without the loss of our values, even if they take different forms than in

---

92 Minutes of the CMER Management Council, 15 May 2000, Foyer Grebel Archive, Centre Mennonite de Paris, France.

93 Christine de Coninck, "Proposition de développement de la M.M.F.," undated, Foyer Grebel Archive, Centre Mennonite de Paris, France.

94 Ibid.

The sheltered workshop at Châtenay-Malabry expanded dramatically over the years. In 2011 it adopted the name Fondation des Amis de l'Atelier and in 2015 represented a network of more than sixty establishments in the Paris region and central France.

the time of our founders."[95] Thus, the council advocated for the latter course. They recognized that some questions remained unresolved—about the spiritual dimension of the association's work, and MMF's future relationship with the French Mennonite community

and its existing partners; they encouraged members to consider the choice over the following year.

In June 2002, the MMF general assembly officially approved the executive council's proposal. This decision would permit MMF to develop its social ministries with financial and legal transparency vis-à-vis the French state, and would free CMER to pursue its desired objectives with complete autonomy. For both parties, the step involved a change of name. Mission Mennonite Française became Association Domaine Emmanuel and then the Association d'Établissements du Domaine Emmanuel (AEDE; Association of Establishments of Domaine Emmanuel). As Victor Dos Santos acknowledged in *Christ Seul*, "For many, the abandonment of the words 'mission' and 'Mennonite' has been difficult." However, he assured his readers, this did not "signify the abandonment of our Christian identity or a desire to distance ourselves from the Mennonite world. Our Christian identity remains present in the word 'Emmanuel,' a reminder of the presence of God [made evident] through our actions."[96] For its part, CMER became Centre Mennonite de Paris (CMP;

---

95 Ibid.

96 Victor Dos Santos, "Un nom nouvel!" *Christ Seul*, April 2003, 22.

Paris Mennonite Center). This more easily translatable name strengthened associations between the work in Paris and that of other Mennonite centers around the world.[97]

Blough's reaction to the MMF general assembly's decision encapsulated the sentiments of both MMF and MBM. Despite the many fruits of past collaboration, the comprehensive nature of the partners' earlier joint work, which combined evangelistic witness with service to the community's social needs, was no longer consonant with French legal structures or with the partners' distinct objectives. Thus, Blough believed, "The development of the Center and of MMF indicates that the moment has arrived for [their separation]. We do not do the same things [and] our methods of financing and functioning are very different. We consider this a normal and desirable development that by no means signifies that the links between the two associations will cease to exist."[98]

After forty-nine years of partnership in mission, the relationship between MMF and Mennonite Mission Network ended in late 2003 in a meeting at Domaine Emmanuel between Robert Charles, Joël Haldemann, and Victor Dos Santos.[99] There, AEDE representatives made the Saint Maurice property available to the Centre Mennonite de Paris rent free for a period of fifty years, provided that the occupants would cover property taxes and insurance. Charles, on MMN's behalf, promised to write a letter putting an end to any existing protocols between the French and North American organizations.[100]

97 Neal Blough, "Le CMER devient le Centre Mennonite de Paris," *Christ Seul*, February 2003, 19.

98 Neal Blough, "Centre Mennonite d'Études et de Rencontre," in the Annual Report of the MMF General Assembly 2002, 20, personal files of Robert Witmer, Cambridge, ON.

99 Mennonite Mission Network (MMN) superseded Mennonite Board of Missions in February 2002 after North American Mennonite conference restructuring.

100 Minutes of meeting attended by Robert Charles (MBM), Joël Haldemann, and Victor Dos Santos (AEDE), 3 November 2003, Foyer Grebel Archive, Centre Mennonite de Paris, France.

5
Conclusion
An Intercultural Partnership's Legacy and Lessons

This book's central purpose has been to describe an experiment in missionary partnership that stimulated intercultural collaboration. In the process, this account has sought to address a number of issues. How did Mission Mennonite Française and Mennonite Board of Missions work with each other? What was their basic approach, and how did they adapt to changing circumstances? What challenges did they face, and how did they overcome them? In answering these questions, this book has detailed the origins and development of the partners' numerous projects, each a unique manifestation of these organizations' shared motivations and missionary strategies. A brief look at those institutions that continue to function today gives one indication of the partnership's success, their growth and longevity testifying to the ongoing relevance of their work. This survey will also engender an

appreciation of a few of the ripple effects of MMF and MBM efforts.

The partnership between Mission Mennonite Française and Mennonite Board of Missions ran its course during a postwar period marked by reestablishment of relationships between North American and European Mennonites. On an official level, attempts by representatives of both groups to interact with each other in mutually beneficial ways met with mixed success. On occasion, North American agencies demonstrated a lack of prudence and sensitivity, pursuing their own goals while ignoring the input of their European counterparts. As a consequence, European Mennonites sometimes displayed a certain distrust of North American motivations. Undoubtedly, however, the general trend in these relationships moved toward greater

Église Évangélique Mennonite of Lamorlaye, north of Paris

understanding, openness, and collaboration.[1] Nowhere was such cooperation more intimate and long lasting, more fruitful and institutionalized, than in France.

Above all, these partners cooperated in order to plant churches. Three Mennonite congregations in the Paris region—Foyer Fraternel in Châtenay-Malabry, Église Protestante Mennonite of Villeneuve-le-Comte (formerly Communauté Chrétienne du Foyer Grebel), and Église Évangélique Mennonite of Lamorlaye—were born as a result of the cooperative efforts of MMF and MBM personnel and of the many people whom they inspired to join them.[2] The impact of these congregations on the lives of their members and their communities is, in many respects, inestimable. There is not space here to record the testimonies of the hundreds of individuals whose lives were touched and transformed by these churches' ministries. However, the congregations' significance to the broader French Mennonite

1 Neal Blough, "Mission Efforts in Europe: New Congregations, New Questions," in *Testing Faith and Tradition*, ed. John A. Lapp and C. Arnold Snyder (Intercourse, PA: Good Books, 2006), 251.

2 Foyer Fraternel convened in the same building from 1958 to 2012. The congregation moved into a larger facility on the same site in 2015. Église Protestante Mennonite of Villeneuve-le-Comte moved to this small town east of Paris in 2003, benefiting from an AEDE loan of more than €200,000 made available from the proceeds of the association's sale of their property in Verrières-le-Buisson. Église Évangélique Mennonite of Lamorlaye, founded in 1997, also found a permanent home in this town just north of Paris in the former chapel of the European Bible Institute, which closed in 2003. For details about the relocations of the Mennonite churches of Villeneuve-le-Comte and Lamorlaye, see Minutes of the Executive Council of MMF, 28 April 2003, AEDE Archive, Hautefeuille, France.

church is more easily measurable. Foyer Fraternel and Communauté Chrétienne du Foyer Grebel were among the first urban Mennonite churches in France.[3] As a result, they were forced to deal with economic, social, and spiritual realities that French Mennonite congregations in the country had not confronted. Their geographical separation from bases of Mennonite ethnicity and tradition, and their overtly evangelistic purposes, led them to adopt a more open disposition to French society than that of some rural, "family-church" congregations in the eastern part of France.[4] These urban churches had to actively tackle the question of what it means to be Mennonite, both theologically and practically. The attempts of Parisian congregations and their leaders to answer this question helped shape diverse ministries of mission, service, and theological reflection that have had a direct impact in shaping the recent development of the French Mennonite church.

Already in the early 1960s, MMF and MBM determined that the conditions they encountered in France

Young members of the Protestant Mennonite Church at Ville-neuve-le-Compte, east of Paris. Photo taken from congregational website in 2015

demanded a comprehensive missionary response to the spiritual, social, and physical needs of their community. The sheltered workshops of Les Amis de l'Atelier and Domaine Emmanuel were concrete expressions of this belief. While Robert Witmer later described the partners' support of services for individuals with

---

3 Blough, "Mission Efforts in Europe," 253.

4 Diether Götz Lichdi, "Mennonites in France," in *Testing Faith and Tradition*, ed. John A. Lapp and C. Arnold Snyder (Intercourse, PA: Good Books, 2006), 176.

developmental disabilities as "the natural and logical consequence of the gospel we preach as disciples," neither he nor his congregation nor his sponsoring agencies could have anticipated how these efforts would later multiply.[5] Primarily under the directorship of Ernest Nussbaumer, Les Amis de l'Atelier has experienced exponential growth and now runs more than sixty establishments and services in the region around Paris and in the department of Haute-Vienne in central France. The Association des Établissements du Domaine Emmanuel, primarily under Victor Dos Santos's leadership, has expanded with similar speed. The organization now operates twelve centers east of Paris in the departments of Seine-et-Marne and Seine-Saint-Denis. Both associations serve hundreds of teenagers, adults, and seniors with disabilities with state-funded annual budgets that run into the tens of millions of euros.

These organizations no longer characterize their work as missionary. Nevertheless, many Mennonite members of their staff and administration continue to attend the Mennonite congregations in Paris and view their service to workers and residents with disabilities as a response to Christ's call to discipleship. Because of the rapid proliferation of their establishments, these organizations represent the greatest point of contact between the institutional fruits of MMF and MBM partnership and French society. Like other French Mennonite social institutions, Les Amis de l'Atelier and AEDE have participated in the postwar renewal of the French Mennonite church by encouraging greater social engagement[6] and by increasing sensitivity and attention to the "welfare of the city."[7] These projects have helped to turn a relatively small Mennonite constituency into the biggest sponsor of social action among evangelicals in the country.[8]

The unique circumstances that MMF and MBM encountered in France spurred reflection about how best to shape an appropriate missionary response to a

5 Robert Witmer to Peter Dyck, 29 June 1982. Box 10, Folder 33. Mennonite Board of Missions Overseas Ministry Division Data Files Part 6, 1980–1984. IV/18/013-06. Mennonite Church USA Archives. Goshen, IN.

6 Michel Paret, "L'Action Sociale Mennonite en France au XX° Siècle: Approches Diachronique et Analytique" (PhD diss., École Pratique des Hautes Études, Sorbonne, Paris, 1997), 268.

7 Michel Sommer, "Les Amis de l'Atelier: 1961–2001," Christ Seul, August/September 2001, 22–30.

8 Paret, "L'Action Sociale Mennonite," 9.

European context in which Christianity was increasingly marginal. This reflection tended to be collaborative, the product of dialogue between individuals from diverse cultural and confessional backgrounds. The staff of the Paris Mennonite Center carry on this work, not introspectively but in an evangelistic manner, seeking to share the results of theological, missiological, and historical study and dialogue with Mennonites and non-Mennonites, both inside and outside France. The center's establishment and ongoing operation demonstrates a commitment to think seriously about the central issues facing the church.[9] Its library, publications, and support of academic training have made Anabaptist Mennonite theology more readily available in both ecumenical and secular contexts. Its staff's teaching and reflection continue to draw attention to the need for Christians to act and think in ways that foster building community, peace, and social justice, and that oppose pervasive racism and violence. The influence of the center's work has spread beyond France through its active participation in the Mennonite World Conference francophone network. As it has since the inauguration of the Foyer Grebel student residence, the Mennonite center in Saint Maurice continues to serve as a gathering place where European, North American, and African Mennonites can meet for fellowship and dialogue.

This brief review of the ongoing work of these projects only hints at the myriad ways in which the fruits of partnership continue to emerge in diverse contexts. The benefits of cooperative action across cultural and linguistic borders and between numerous individuals and organizations seem clear. Yet, if this particular history has value, it is found in the description of a specific missionary partnership lived out in a specific set of circumstances. This account permits the observation of partnership in practice. Thus, alongside an enumeration of the benefits of cooperation in mission, this study has honestly described the challenges that are engendered by intercultural collaboration. While it is not the historian's principal task to draw lessons from the past, it is possible here to highlight a few of the central issues that shaped the partners' relationship and activity.

---

9 Alan Kreider, "West Europe in Missional Perspective: Themes from Mennonite Mission, 1950–2004," in *Evangelical, Ecumenical, and Anabaptist Missiologies in Conversation: Essays in Honor of Wilbert R. Shenk*, ed. James R. Krabill, Walter Sawatsky, and Charles E. Van Engen (Maryknoll, NY: Orbis, 2006), 211.

First, this partnership history demonstrates the power of joint projects to bring distanced groups closer together. The relationship between MMF and MBM experienced its greatest intimacy, growth, and maturation in the periods of time in which new projects were founded. Discussions about personnel and sources of financing forged common objectives and opened channels of communication. Successful attempts to solve problems created trust and increased comfort with mutual dependency. Practical, hands-on work brought people into close contact with one another, encouraging greater appreciation for common interests and diverse perspectives. The benefits of shared participation in mission work were not limited to representatives of MMF or MBM. Pax involvement in the work of the Paris mission prompted collaboration between North American mission and service agencies that often found it difficult to cooperate with one another. The partners' activities also stimulated greater unity among French Mennonites. This was evident in the diverse composition of the executive council and general assembly of MMF itself. Furthermore, regular meetings, building dedications, and work camps brought German- and French-speaking Mennonites from eastern France together with their new brothers and sisters in Paris, leading to the formation of lasting friendships that continue to affect the way French, North American, and African Mennonites understand one another and their common faith.

Second, this partnership history reveals the importance of strong organizational structures that clarify roles, facilitate communication, and formalize accountability. If this history has focused intently on the development of these frameworks over the course of the partnership, it is because when they failed or were absent, relationships easily deteriorated, confidence eroded, and organizational bonds became more vulnerable to individual weaknesses or interpersonal conflicts. On the whole, the partnership between MMF and MBM benefited when representatives of both organizations understood their roles and responsibilities and carried them out to the best of their abilities. Certainly, this was not always the case. For example, at times MBM struggled to determine to what degree it should intervene in the supervision of its missionaries and their activities in France. This task was complicated by the occasional failure of MMF to exert its supervisory authority over the board's missionary personnel. Significant problems arose when the partnership's organizational framework broke down. Yet, both partners demonstrated an ongoing willingness to restructure the terms of their relationship in response to changing conditions.

Conversely, the relationships between the congregations the partners had founded and the projects to which these faith communities were linked were often inadequately defined. To a degree, this dynamic grew out of the missionaries' commitment to Anabaptist ecclesiology, which encouraged the creation of tight-knit communities that pursued a wide variety of evangelistic and service activities in close collaboration. This community model promoted close physical proximity of people and projects and generated intense inter-personal relationships. At times, such arrangements helped members of these congregations to better understand God's call to discipleship and created unique opportunities for them to testify to God's love. Yet, all too often, these conditions fostered the development of unhealthy and damaging power dynamics, with individuals occupying numerous positions of authority in different organizations. The painful separation of Les Amis de l'Atelier from Foyer Fraternel and that of CMER from Communauté Chrétienne du Foyer

Joint worship of the three Mennonite congregations in the Paris region

Grebel were the unfortunate result of unrealistic assumptions about the possibilities for close integration between churches and associated projects.

Third, this partnership history reveals the effects of sources of funding on the character and objectives of missionary projects. After the opening of the sheltered workshop in Châtenay-Malabry, the partners drew on two sources of financial support for the development of their projects: (1) the donations, loans, and offerings of French and North American Mennonites and (2) public funds. These diverse sources of support allowed MMF to develop a variety of evangelism and service programs, each of which formed one part of a comprehensive missionary witness. The partnership's unique mobilization of state money, a first both for French Mennonites and for MBM, offered financial stability to the partners' ministry to youth with developmental disabilities, which likely would not have survived without it. However, over time, these state-funded institutions were obligated to conform to the demands of their funders. Public money allowed them to provide increasingly professionalized service, but it eroded the overtly missionary quality of their action. The professionalization of their care, the increased complexity of their administration, and the urgent demand to offer more services resulted in an inevitable distancing of the social projects from the constituencies and congregations that had founded, staffed, and supported them. After gaining their independence from church oversight, often in conflictual circumstances, they developed their own identity, largely separate from the church.

Although many had regrets about this course of events, most saw it as inevitable. How could churches effectively supervise or administer institutions that they did not fund and for which they had no legal responsibility? In light of this reality, a 1994 CMER report, commissioned by the national French Mennonite church to address this issue, recommended that official ties between congregations and social institutions—which constrained the independent decision-making processes of both groups—be broken. The report's authors, Frédéric de Coninck and Neal Blough, suggested that healthier and more productive links between Mennonite churches and social projects could be nurtured through forums for informal discussion and fostered by communication between individuals participating in the administrative bodies of congregations and social projects.[10] This has been the course along which relations between the church and Mennonite social institutions have developed. Many ties have been maintained,

---

10 Neal Blough and Frédéric de Coninck, "La Mise en Oeuvre du Salut," May 1994, in Paret, "L'Action Sociale Mennonite," Annexes, 102.

but they are no longer financial or administrative. While this model may not have been what MMF and MBM initially envisioned, its emergence results from the approaches adopted by the partners decades ago.

Fortunately, these social projects and the French Mennonite church have recently expressed greater desire to strengthen the tenuous bonds that link them together. Writing in the June 2012 issue of *Christ Seul*, current Association d'Établissements du Domaine Emmanuel director André Hege offered an assessment of the state of these two groups' relationship and laid out possibilities for the development of stronger ties. Speaking on behalf of Les Amis de l'Atelier, the homes at Valdoie and Mont des Oiseaux, and his own organization, Hege suggested that after periods during which these institutions had experienced dependence on and independence from the church, the time had arrived for greater interdependence. He called for increased communication between social projects and churches through the pages of *Christ Seul* and through representatives, designated in each congregation, who would relay information between these entities. He also drew attention to a recent agreement between the newly created association of Mennonite social institutions and the Association des Églises Évangéliques Mennonites de France that promised to establish shared objectives.[11] Thus, it appeared that MMF and MBM projects were moving back to a model of collaboration, but one that sought to avoid the pitfalls of the recent past.

As Hege's article demonstrates, much has changed since French and North American Mennonites began their partnership in mission in the 1950s. For one thing, the pioneering model of intercultural cooperation in mission is no longer rare. In the past decades, the growth of Mennonite World Conference has permitted Mennonites from around the world to build relationships with one another and to think together in new ways about international missionary collaboration. Still, many of the challenges inherent in working together across cultural and linguistic barriers, in sharing gifts and perspectives, remain. This reality is a central reason why the history of partnership between MMF and MBM remains relevant.

It is important to remember that those who developed this unique model in France had no master template to follow. As a result, the partners faced numerous

11 André Hege, "Églises et Oeuvres: Cultivons nos Liens!" *Christ Seul*, June 2012, 36.

challenges as they sought to follow God's missionary call together. Most often, moments of difficulty served as occasions for growth, for the clear and powerful manifestation of God's guidance. At other times, individual or institutional relationships were damaged. Nevertheless, as Allen Koop observes in his study of postwar evangelical missions in France, no other missionary project in the country during the latter half of the twentieth century fostered cooperation as close and as productive as that carried out by French and North American Mennonites. No other mission succeeded in combining evangelism and church planting with significant social work to the same degree. No other mission demonstrated the same openness to collaborating with outside groups and agencies, including the French state.[12]

The achievements of this partnership are attributable both to MBM's desire to assist rather than compete with French Mennonites, and to the hospitable and cooperative attitude exhibited by their French Mennonite hosts and coworkers. As Neal Blough explains,

The ministry in Hautefeuille expanded rapidly and in 2002 adopted the name Association of Establishments of Domaine Emmanuel. AEDE now operates twelve centers located east of Paris.

"There were already congregations and institutions in existence of which we could become a part. There were already people there who could help us understand the context, people who could teach us and give counsel, encourage us, and help us find our place. From the beginning, we were surrounded by people who already knew the context and were open to collaborate with foreigners."[13] While the partners' common action was

---

12 Allen V. Koop, *American Evangelical Missionaries in France 1945–1975* (Lanham, MD: University Press of America, 1986), 91.

13 Blough, "Mission in Europe," 217.

founded on trust in each other, a more basic conviction underlay their willingness to enter unfamiliar territory together. Most evident in the name "Emmanuel," chosen by Robert Witmer and André Kennel for the sheltered workshop in Hautefeuille, it was the partners' shared belief that they had already entered into partnership with God, who was and would always be present with them, that encouraged them to enter into partnership with each other.

Index

About the Author

David Y. Neufeld studies early Anabaptist history as a PhD candidate in The Division for Late Medieval and Reformation Studies at the University of Arizona. He and his wife, Gina Martinez, currently attend Shalom Mennonite Fellowship in Tucson.